HEROES OF HISTORY

MAPS

of the
United States

A Reproducible Workbook
and Curriculum Guide

Emerald Books

P.O. BOX 635, LYNNWOOD, WA 98046

Emerald Books are distributed through YWAM Publishing. For a full list of titles, visit our website at www.ywampublishing.com or call 1-800-922-2143.

Maps of the United States

12 11 10 09 08 07 06 05   10 9 8 7 6 5 4 3 2 1

Published by Emerald Books
P.O. Box 635
Lynnwood, Washington 98046

ISBN 1-932096-26-4

Printed in the United States of America.

Contents

INTRODUCTION 4

EXPLORING THE UNITED STATES 6
United States of America
The Fifty States: Alabama, Alaska, Arizona, Arkansas, California, Colorado, Connecticut, Delaware, Florida, Georgia, Hawaii, Idaho, Illinois, Indiana, Iowa, Kansas, Kentucky, Louisiana, Maine, Maryland, Massachusetts, Michigan, Minnesota, Mississippi, Missouri, Montana, Nebraska, Nevada, New Hampshire, New Jersey, New Mexico, New York, North Carolina, North Dakota, Ohio, Oklahoma, Oregon, Pennsylvania, Rhode Island, South Carolina, South Dakota, Tennessee, Texas, Utah, Vermont, Virginia, Washington, West Virginia, Wisconsin, Wyoming
Washington, D.C.

APPENDIX A: HISTORICAL MAPPING ACTIVITIES 109
The Thirteen Colonies and the American Revolution
The Louisiana Purchase
The Civil War

APPENDIX B: ADDITIONAL MAPPING ACTIVITIES FOR THE UNITED STATES 116

APPENDIX C: STUDENT EXPLORATIONS 118

APPENDIX D: CONCEPTUAL SOCIAL STUDIES EXERCISES 121

APPENDIX E: RESOURCES 122

EXTRA UNITED STATES MAP 128

Introduction

Designed for use in schools and homeschools, *Maps of the United States* is a reproducible resource suitable for students of a variety of ages, abilities, and learning styles. The student worksheets and maps may be duplicated for use by more than one student.* Or one student can work directly in the workbook, so that in the end he or she has a bound reference book and keepsake of his or her mapping work and fact sheets.

At the prompting of teachers* who use the Heroes of History biography series by Janet and Geoff Benge in their school and homeschool curriculum, we at Emerald Books have prepared this unique collection of hand-drawn maps, worksheets, and activities that further support the study of the United States and its history. While this workbook is an excellent companion to the Heroes of History series, it stands alone and doesn't in any way require that you use the biographies.

Reproducible state maps and worksheets. At the heart of *Maps of the United States* are the reproducible maps and worksheets for the fifty states. Included with these are a map and worksheet for the entire United States as well as a worksheet for our nation's one district, the District of Columbia. The state worksheets are designed to initiate a student's research. They are identical so that students gather parallel information about all fifty states. Students will learn about such things as the date of statehood, state population and area, and major exports. The worksheets also contain a list of items to locate and label on the facing map, including geographical features and major cities. Major rivers, lakes, and mountain ranges are indicated on the state maps but are not labeled.

The worksheets and maps for the fifty states are arranged alphabetically for ease in locating them, since teachers will have different methods of teaching about the states. Even if you use the book as a workbook for a single student, you can of course direct him or her to complete the activities in a different sequence, for example, by date of entry into the Union or by regional groupings. Because the worksheets and maps are reproducible, these pages are not numbered.

In addition to the state maps and worksheets, *Maps of the United States* contains many other helps for studying the the fifty states.

Historical mapping activities. The additional maps and mapping instructions in Appendix A allow the student to learn more about the history of the United States through mapping activities related to the Thirteen Colonies, the American Revolution, the Louisiana Purchase, and the Civil War. These pages are designed to be used by the student. However, the maps will be useful even if you choose to modify the mapping directions according to the student's study of these historical periods.

Additional mapping activities for the United States. A resource for the teacher, Appendix B contains additional mapping activities that help students explore both the historical and contemporary United States. We've included an extra copy of the map of the United States at the end of the book. We suggest that you keep this as a spare to duplicate for additional mapping activities, such as those suggested in this appendix.

Student explorations. Appendix C contains many diverse activities from which you can choose, providing students of different ages, abilities, and learning styles with the forum to delve deeper into learning about the fifty states as well as the nation's capital and U.S. dependencies. Suggested activities include report writing, creative writing, oral presentations, and hands-on activities like three-dimensional map modeling and creating timelines, brochures, and children's books. The activities require a varying amount of research and can be made more or less comprehensive at your discretion. Choose the activities that are best suited to your student or students.

Conceptual social studies exercises. The conceptual social studies exercises in Appendix D involve activities like comparing state areas and populations and studying maps of precipitation and population density. Students can engage these exercises through group discussions, paragraph writing, or short oral reports.

Resources. Appendix E describes some of the many good resources available for studying the fifty states. The featured resources include books, Internet sites, and subscription sites available free of charge through many libraries and schools.

Student instructions. In addition to the flexibility of choosing which activities to do, which states to cover, and what order to follow, this workbook gives you the freedom to provide specific instructions for the worksheet and mapping activities, recognizing that this will depend on a student's grade level and learning goals.

It is our hope that the stylized, hand-drawn maps will encourage creativity and craftsmanship in the student's own work. Depending on their learning objectives, students may benefit from specific guidelines for using color, how to mark the different features (such as national parks) and how to label the various classes of items (such as rivers, states, capital cities, and other cities). Students of all ages may need a reminder to be aware of the locations of all items they are mapping before they actually begin so that they can use the space well and create a clean, attractive map. Younger students especially may want to write their labels in light pencil first.

To supplement the favorite resources you may already use, Appendix E refers you to many good sources of the information required for the worksheets and mapping activities. Students may also enjoy studying several examples of published maps, both historical and contemporary, to become familiar with mapping conventions and styles.

Here are a few explanations you may want to pass on: (1) Because the state worksheets are identical, students should be alerted that not every state has every feature listed in the mapping directions. For example, there are no mountain ranges in Iowa. As students gather their mapping data and discover that a feature is missing, they will have learned something about the state. (2) Students may need explanations of the items on the worksheets. For example, they are directed to map the state's major geographical regions. In Maryland, these are the Atlantic Coastal Plain, Piedmont, Blue Ridge, Appalachian Ridge and Valley, and Appalachian Plateau. Descriptions of a state's regions are readily available in encyclopedias and other resources. (3) Although the individual state maps do not show the bordering lands or waters, students can still label these in the white space around the map. If students map the United States first, they can refer to their own map to see the states' locations and bordering states. The U.S. worksheet and map precede those of the fifty states.

One of our goals for the Heroes of History biographies has been to create a panorama of American history that makes history come alive to young people through the lives of influential people. This complementary addition to the Heroes of History series provides another creative vehicle for learning about the United States and its history, this time through the fifty fascinating states of the Union. We hope that you and your students enjoy the journey.

---

*For the sake of brevity in the instructions, the word *teacher* includes the homeschooling parent and the word *student* refers to a child either in a traditional classroom or in a homeschool environment.

Gather these facts about the United States, filling in the blanks.

Official name _____ Capital _____

Date of independence _____ Type of government _____

Current population _____ World rank in population _____

Land area _____ Water area _____ World rank in area _____
        (square miles)   *(square miles)*

Highest point _____ Lowest point _____

Six largest cities and their populations _____

_____

_____

Gross domestic product (GDP) _____ Per capita GDP _____

Major industries _____

_____

Chief agricultural products _____

_____

Major exports _____

_____

Major imports _____

_____

Map It!

Gather the following information and mark each item on the blank map of the United States.

- The fifty states
- The capital city of each state
- The nation's capital and former capitals
- The nations and bodies of water that border the United States

Decorate the banner with the state's name and gather these facts about the state, filling in the blanks.

Date of statehood _____ Rank of entry into union _____ of 50

State motto _____

State nickname _____

Origin of state name _____

_____

Current population _____ Rank in population _____ of 50

Land area _____ Water area _____ Rank in total area _____ of 50
      (square miles)   *(square miles)*

Major natural resources _____

Major industries _____

Major exports _____

Governor _____ Number of representatives elected to U.S. Congress _____

U.S. senators _____

State abbreviation (e.g., Ariz.) _____ Postal code (e.g., AZ) _____

Name for resident of this state (e.g., Californian) _____

Map It!

Research the following geographical features. Then mark each item on the blank map of the state.

- The state's major rivers and bodies of water
- The state's mountain ranges
- The highest point in the state and its elevation
- The state's capital city
- The state's five largest cities
- The state's geographical regions
- National parks in the state
- Any other special geographical features (e.g., Washington's volcanic Mount Saint Helens)
- Bordering states, nations (if Canada, specify province), and bodies of water

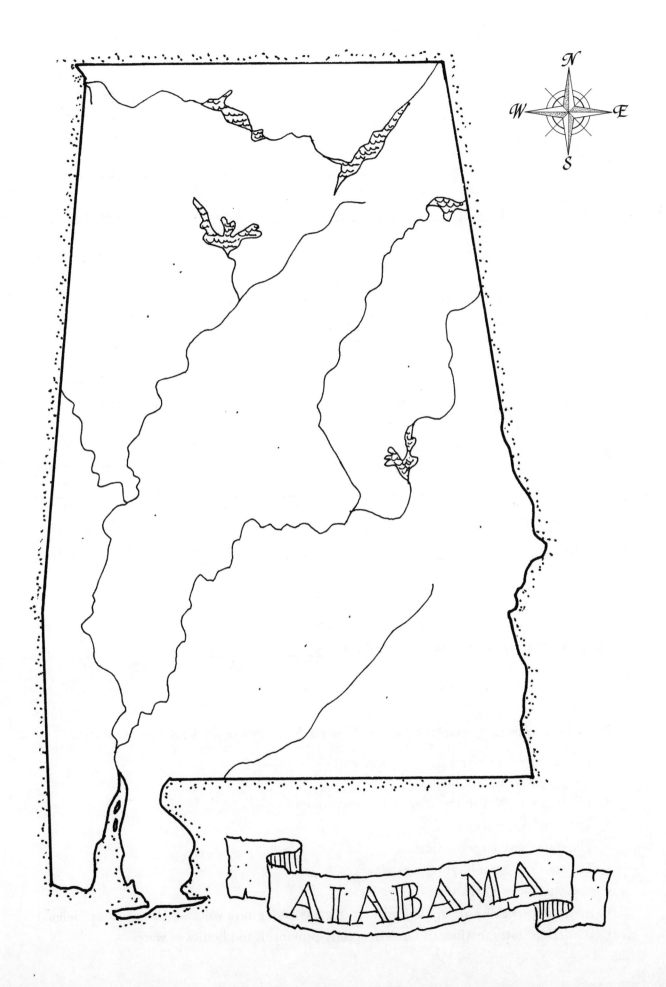

Decorate the banner with the state's name and gather these facts about the state, filling in the blanks.

Date of statehood _____ Rank of entry into union _____ of 50

State motto _____

State nickname _____

Origin of state name _____

_____

Current population _____ Rank in population _____ of 50

Land area _____ Water area _____ Rank in total area _____ of 50
      (square miles)   *(square miles)*

Major natural resources _____

Major industries _____

Major exports _____

Governor _____ Number of representatives elected to U.S. Congress _____

U.S. senators _____

State abbreviation (e.g., Ariz.) _____ Postal code (e.g., AZ) _____

Name for resident of this state (e.g., Californian) _____

Map It!

Research the following geographical features. Then mark each item on the blank map of the state.

- The state's major rivers and bodies of water
- The state's mountain ranges
- The highest point in the state and its elevation
- The state's capital city
- The state's five largest cities
- The state's geographical regions
- National parks in the state
- Any other special geographical features (e.g., Washington's volcanic Mount Saint Helens)
- Bordering states, nations (if Canada, specify province), and bodies of water

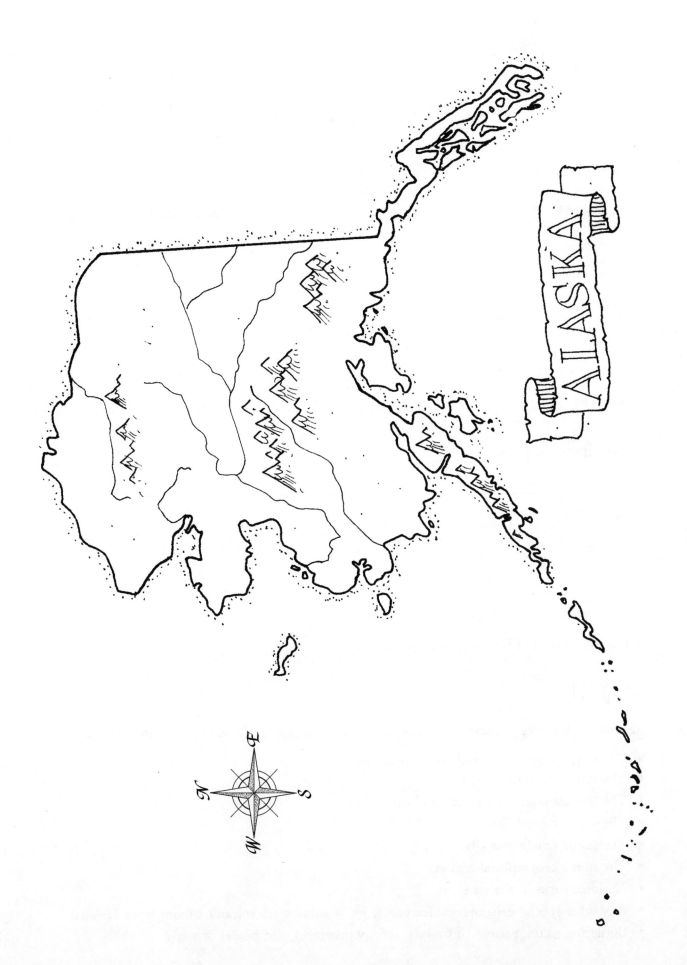

Decorate the banner with the state's name and gather these facts about the state, filling in the blanks.

Date of statehood _____ Rank of entry into union _____ of 50

State motto _____

State nickname _____

Origin of state name _____

_____

Current population _____ Rank in population _____ of 50

Land area _____ Water area _____ Rank in total area _____ of 50

       (square miles)   *(square miles)*

Major natural resources _____

Major industries _____

Major exports _____

Governor _____ Number of representatives elected to U.S. Congress _____

U.S. senators _____

State abbreviation (e.g., Ariz.) _____ Postal code (e.g., AZ) _____

Name for resident of this state (e.g., Californian) _____

Map It!

Research the following geographical features. Then mark each item on the blank map of the state.

- The state's major rivers and bodies of water
- The state's mountain ranges
- The highest point in the state and its elevation
- The state's capital city
- The state's five largest cities
- The state's geographical regions
- National parks in the state
- Any other special geographical features (e.g., Washington's volcanic Mount Saint Helens)
- Bordering states, nations (if Canada, specify province), and bodies of water

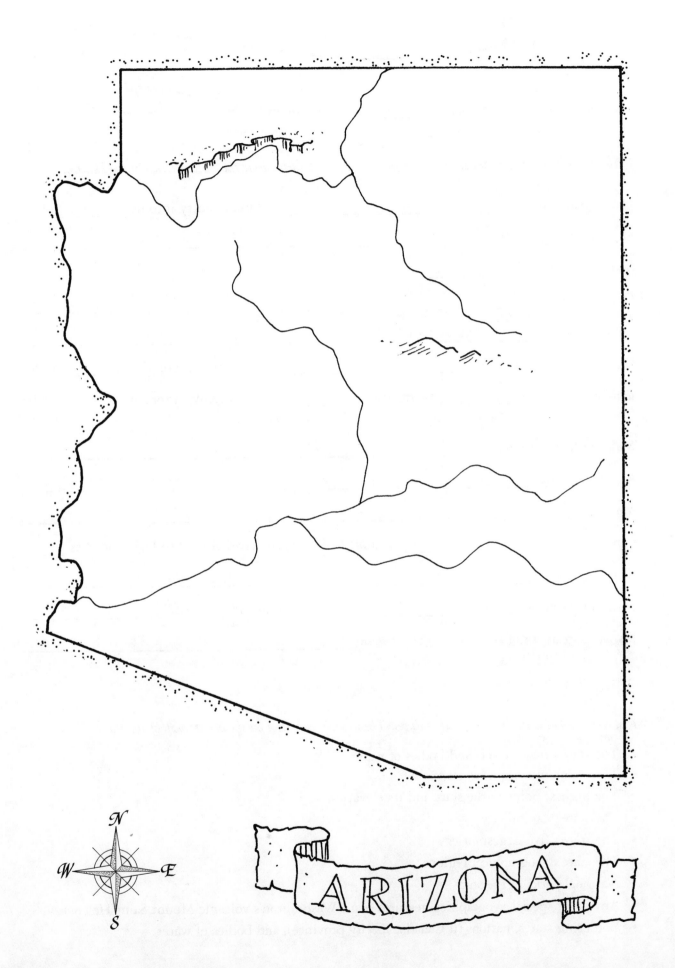

ARIZONA

Decorate the banner with the state's name and gather these facts about the state, filling in the blanks.

Date of statehood _____ Rank of entry into union _____ of 50

State motto _____

State nickname _____

Origin of state name _____

_____

Current population _____ Rank in population _____ of 50

Land area _____ Water area _____ Rank in total area _____ of 50
            (square miles)   *(square miles)*

Major natural resources _____

Major industries _____

Major exports _____

Governor _____ Number of representatives elected to U.S. Congress _____

U.S. senators _____

State abbreviation (e.g., Ariz.) _____ Postal code (e.g., AZ) _____

Name for resident of this state (e.g., Californian) _____

Map It!

Research the following geographical features. Then mark each item on the blank map of the state.

- The state's major rivers and bodies of water
- The state's mountain ranges
- The highest point in the state and its elevation
- The state's capital city
- The state's five largest cities
- The state's geographical regions
- National parks in the state
- Any other special geographical features (e.g., Washington's volcanic Mount Saint Helens)
- Bordering states, nations (if Canada, specify province), and bodies of water

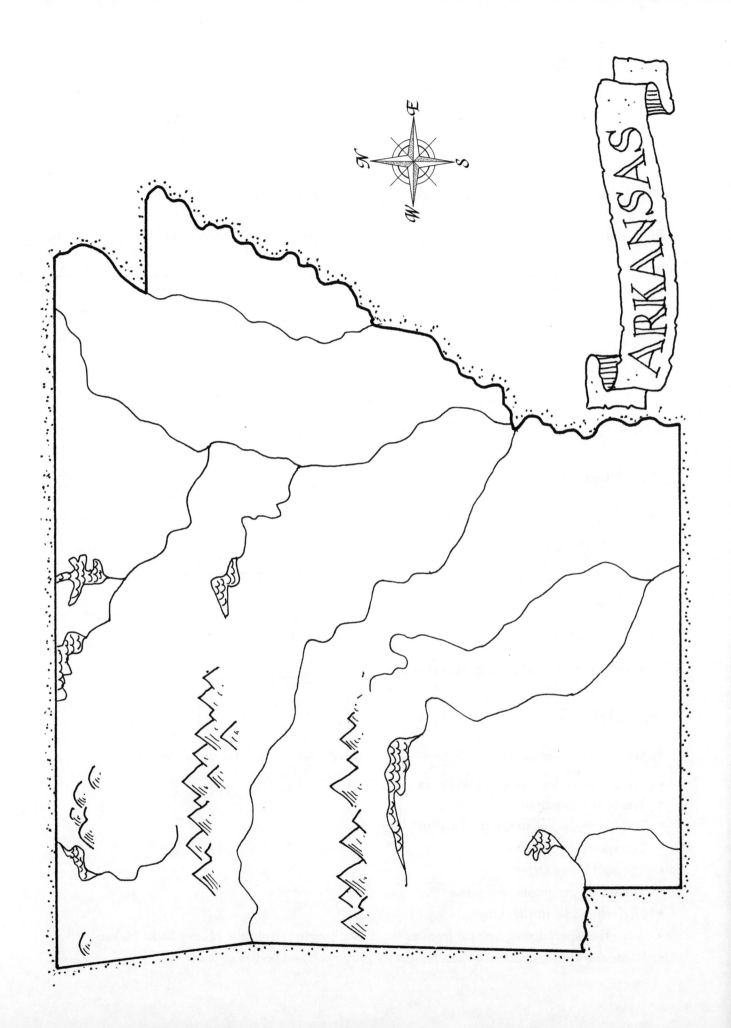

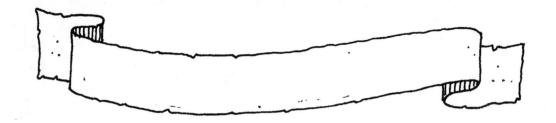

Decorate the banner with the state's name and gather these facts about the state, filling in the blanks.

Date of statehood _____ Rank of entry into union _____ of 50

State motto _____

State nickname _____

Origin of state name _____

_____

Current population _____ Rank in population _____ of 50

Land area _____ Water area _____ Rank in total area _____ of 50
                (square miles)   (square miles)

Major natural resources _____

Major industries _____

Major exports _____

Governor _____ Number of representatives elected to U.S. Congress _____

U.S. senators _____

State abbreviation (e.g., Ariz.) _____ Postal code (e.g., AZ) _____

Name for resident of this state (e.g., Californian) _____

Map It!

Research the following geographical features. Then mark each item on the blank map of the state.

- The state's major rivers and bodies of water
- The state's mountain ranges
- The highest point in the state and its elevation
- The state's capital city
- The state's five largest cities
- The state's geographical regions
- National parks in the state
- Any other special geographical features (e.g., Washington's volcanic Mount Saint Helens)
- Bordering states, nations (if Canada, specify province), and bodies of water

CALIFORNIA

Decorate the banner with the state's name and gather these facts about the state, filling in the blanks.

Date of statehood _____ Rank of entry into union _____ of 50

State motto _____

State nickname _____

Origin of state name _____

_____

Current population _____ Rank in population _____ of 50

Land area _____ Water area _____ Rank in total area _____ of 50
　　　　　　(square miles)　　　　　　　　　　*(square miles)*

Major natural resources _____

Major industries _____

Major exports _____

Governor _____ Number of representatives elected to U.S. Congress _____

U.S. senators _____

State abbreviation (e.g., Ariz.) _____ Postal code (e.g., AZ) _____

Name for resident of this state (e.g., Californian) _____

Map It!

Research the following geographical features. Then mark each item on the blank map of the state.

- The state's major rivers and bodies of water
- The state's mountain ranges
- The highest point in the state and its elevation
- The state's capital city
- The state's five largest cities
- The state's geographical regions
- National parks in the state
- Any other special geographical features (e.g., Washington's volcanic Mount Saint Helens)
- Bordering states, nations (if Canada, specify province), and bodies of water

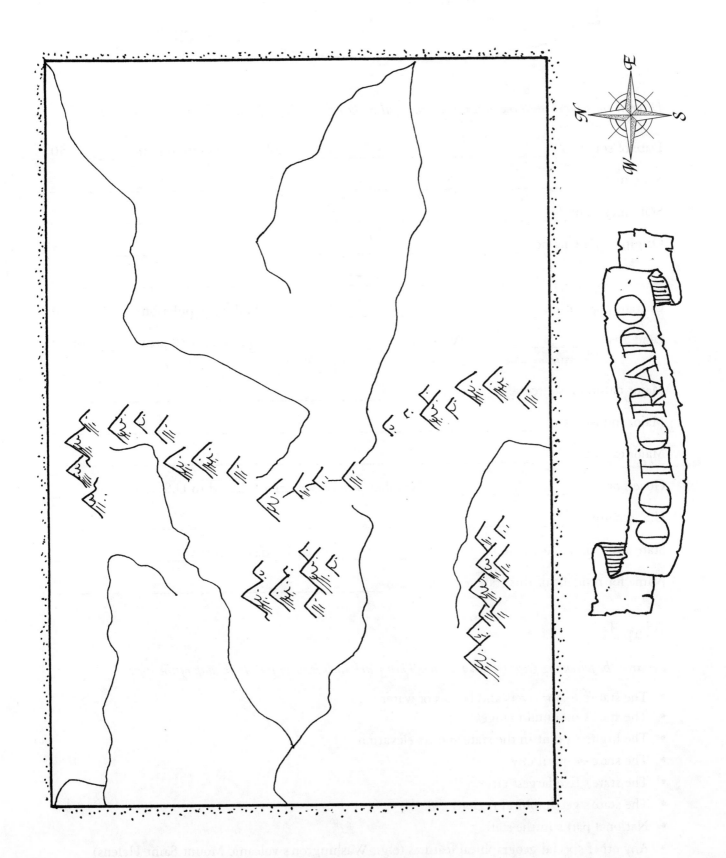

Decorate the banner with the state's name and gather these facts about the state, filling in the blanks.

Date of statehood _____ Rank of entry into union _____ of 50

State motto _____

State nickname _____

Origin of state name _____

_____

Current population _____ Rank in population _____ of 50

Land area _____ Water area _____ Rank in total area _____ of 50
　　　　　(square miles)　　　　　　　　　　(square miles)

Major natural resources _____

Major industries _____

Major exports _____

Governor _____ Number of representatives elected to U.S. Congress _____

U.S. senators _____

State abbreviation (e.g., Ariz.) _____ Postal code (e.g., AZ) _____

Name for resident of this state (e.g., Californian) _____

Map It!

Research the following geographical features. Then mark each item on the blank map of the state.

- The state's major rivers and bodies of water
- The state's mountain ranges
- The highest point in the state and its elevation
- The state's capital city
- The state's five largest cities
- The state's geographical regions
- National parks in the state
- Any other special geographical features (e.g., Washington's volcanic Mount Saint Helens)
- Bordering states, nations (if Canada, specify province), and bodies of water

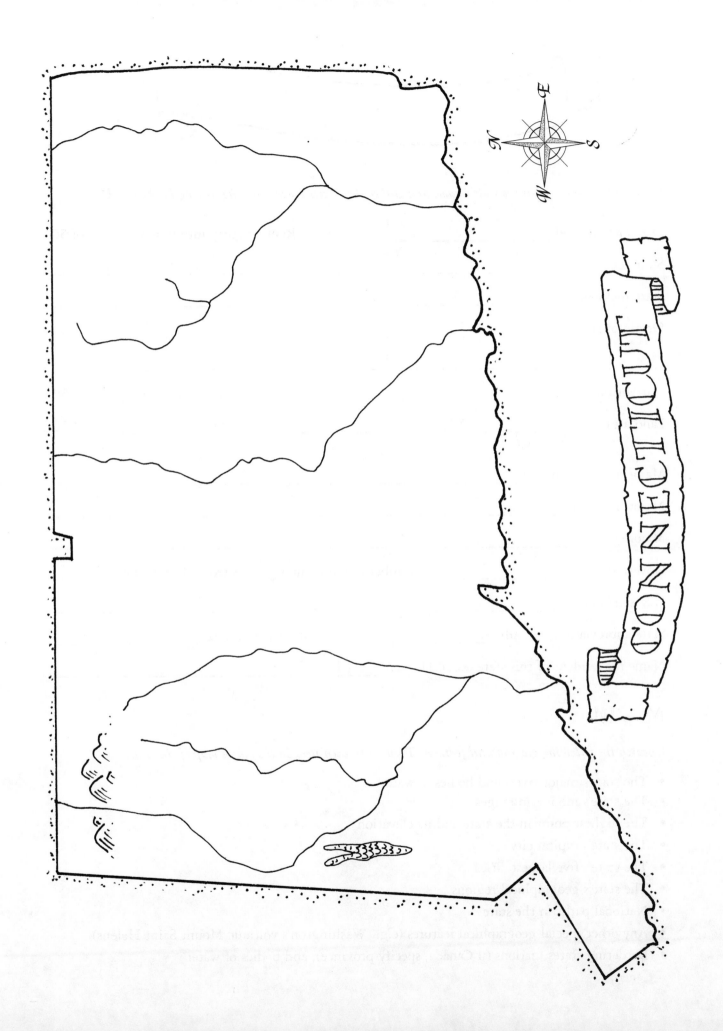

CONNECTICUT

Decorate the banner with the state's name and gather these facts about the state, filling in the blanks.

Date of statehood _____ Rank of entry into union _____ of 50

State motto _____

State nickname _____

Origin of state name _____

_____

Current population _____ Rank in population _____ of 50

Land area _____ Water area _____ Rank in total area _____ of 50
      (square miles)   *(square miles)*

Major natural resources _____

Major industries _____

Major exports _____

Governor _____ Number of representatives elected to U.S. Congress _____

U.S. senators _____

State abbreviation (e.g., Ariz.) _____ Postal code (e.g., AZ) _____

Name for resident of this state (e.g., Californian) _____

Map It!

Research the following geographical features. Then mark each item on the blank map of the state.

- The state's major rivers and bodies of water
- The state's mountain ranges
- The highest point in the state and its elevation
- The state's capital city
- The state's five largest cities
- The state's geographical regions
- National parks in the state
- Any other special geographical features (e.g., Washington's volcanic Mount Saint Helens)
- Bordering states, nations (if Canada, specify province), and bodies of water

Decorate the banner with the state's name and gather these facts about the state, filling in the blanks.

Date of statehood _____ Rank of entry into union _____ of 50

State motto _____

State nickname _____

Origin of state name _____

_____

Current population _____ Rank in population _____ of 50

Land area _____ Water area _____ Rank in total area _____ of 50
      (square miles)   *(square miles)*

Major natural resources _____

Major industries _____

Major exports _____

Governor _____ Number of representatives elected to U.S. Congress _____

U.S. senators _____

State abbreviation (e.g., Ariz.) _____ Postal code (e.g., AZ) _____

Name for resident of this state (e.g., Californian) _____

Map It!

Research the following geographical features. Then mark each item on the blank map of the state.

- The state's major rivers and bodies of water
- The state's mountain ranges
- The highest point in the state and its elevation
- The state's capital city
- The state's five largest cities
- The state's geographical regions
- National parks in the state
- Any other special geographical features (e.g., Washington's volcanic Mount Saint Helens)
- Bordering states, nations (if Canada, specify province), and bodies of water

FLORIDA

Decorate the banner with the state's name and gather these facts about the state, filling in the blanks.

Date of statehood _____ Rank of entry into union _____ of 50

State motto _____

State nickname _____

Origin of state name _____

_____

Current population _____ Rank in population _____ of 50

Land area _____ Water area _____ Rank in total area _____ of 50
  (square miles)   (square miles)

Major natural resources _____

Major industries _____

Major exports _____

Governor _____ Number of representatives elected to U.S. Congress _____

U.S. senators _____

State abbreviation (e.g., Ariz.) _____ Postal code (e.g., AZ) _____

Name for resident of this state (e.g., Californian) _____

Map It!

Research the following geographical features. Then mark each item on the blank map of the state.

- The state's major rivers and bodies of water
- The state's mountain ranges
- The highest point in the state and its elevation
- The state's capital city
- The state's five largest cities
- The state's geographical regions
- National parks in the state
- Any other special geographical features (e.g., Washington's volcanic Mount Saint Helens)
- Bordering states, nations (if Canada, specify province), and bodies of water

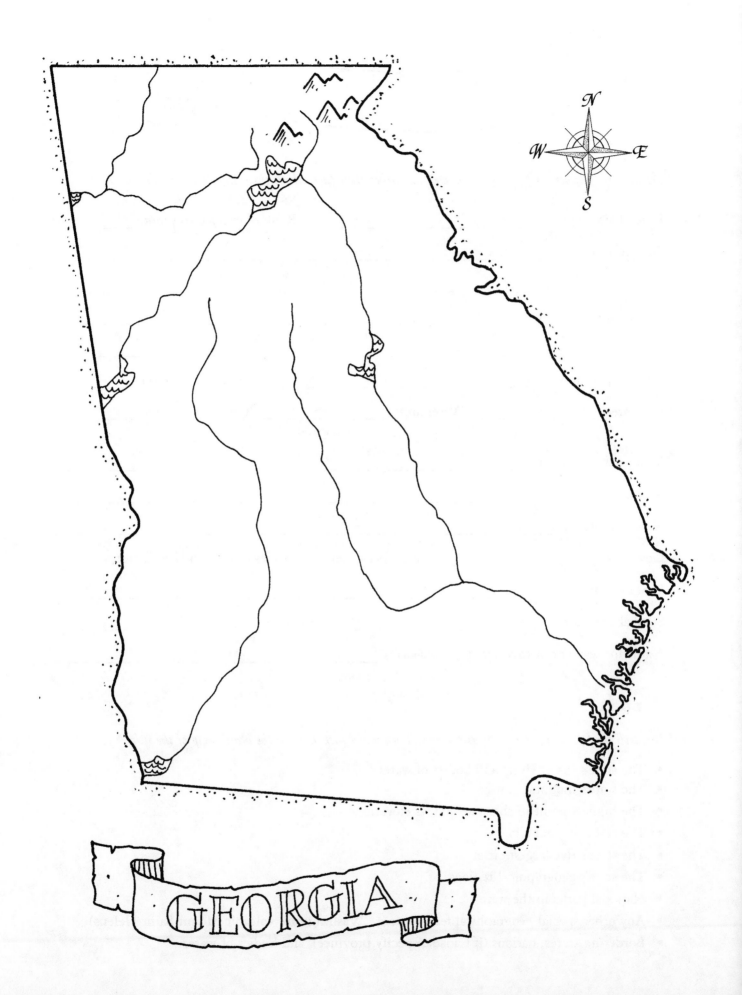

GEORGIA

Decorate the banner with the state's name and gather these facts about the state, filling in the blanks.

Date of statehood _____ Rank of entry into union _____ of 50

State motto _____

State nickname _____

Origin of state name _____

_____

Current population _____ Rank in population _____ of 50

Land area _____ Water area _____ Rank in total area _____ of 50
         (square miles)   *(square miles)*

Major natural resources _____

Major industries _____

Major exports _____

Governor _____ Number of representatives elected to U.S. Congress _____

U.S. senators _____

State abbreviation (e.g., Ariz.) _____ Postal code (e.g., AZ) _____

Name for resident of this state (e.g., Californian) _____

Map It!

Research the following geographical features. Then mark each item on the blank map of the state.

- The state's major rivers and bodies of water
- The state's mountain ranges
- The highest point in the state and its elevation
- The state's capital city
- The state's five largest cities
- The state's geographical regions
- National parks in the state
- Any other special geographical features (e.g., Washington's volcanic Mount Saint Helens)
- Bordering states, nations (if Canada, specify province), and bodies of water

Decorate the banner with the state's name and gather these facts about the state, filling in the blanks.

Date of statehood _____ Rank of entry into union _____ of 50

State motto _____

State nickname _____

Origin of state name _____

_____

Current population _____ Rank in population _____ of 50

Land area _____ Water area _____ Rank in total area _____ of 50
      (square miles)   *(square miles)*

Major natural resources _____

Major industries _____

Major exports _____

Governor _____ Number of representatives elected to U.S. Congress _____

U.S. senators _____

State abbreviation (e.g., Ariz.) _____ Postal code (e.g., AZ) _____

Name for resident of this state (e.g., Californian) _____

Map It!

Research the following geographical features. Then mark each item on the blank map of the state.

- The state's major rivers and bodies of water
- The state's mountain ranges
- The highest point in the state and its elevation
- The state's capital city
- The state's five largest cities
- The state's geographical regions
- National parks in the state
- Any other special geographical features (e.g., Washington's volcanic Mount Saint Helens)
- Bordering states, nations (if Canada, specify province), and bodies of water

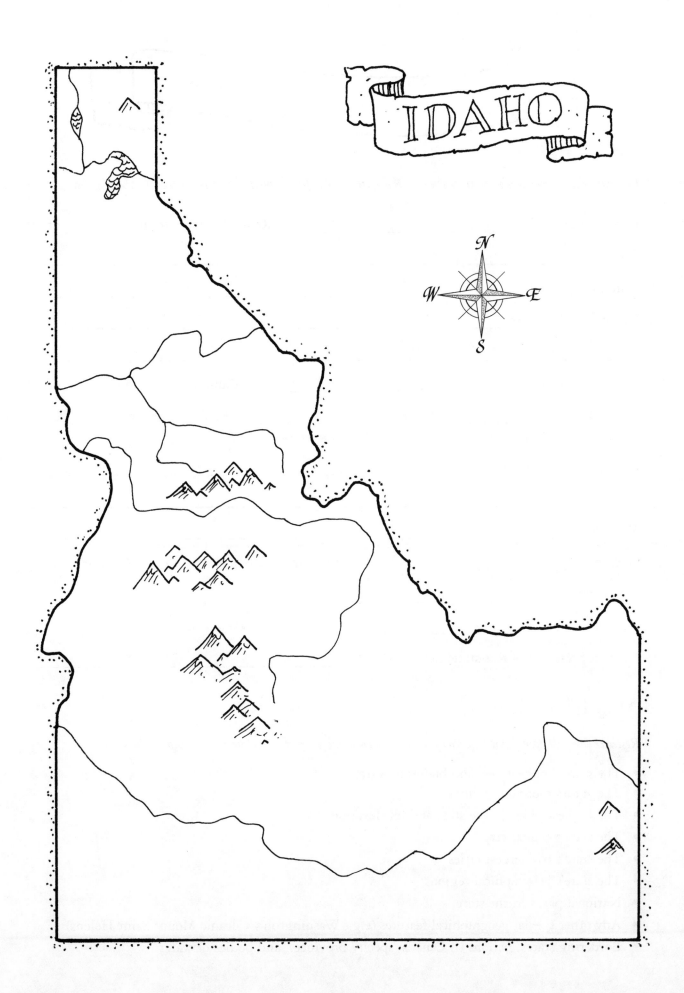

Decorate the banner with the state's name and gather these facts about the state, filling in the blanks.

Date of statehood _____ Rank of entry into union _____ of 50

State motto _____

State nickname _____

Origin of state name _____

_____

Current population _____ Rank in population _____ of 50

Land area _____ Water area _____ Rank in total area _____ of 50
    (square miles)   (square miles)

Major natural resources _____

Major industries _____

Major exports _____

Governor _____ Number of representatives elected to U.S. Congress _____

U.S. senators _____

State abbreviation (e.g., Ariz.) _____ Postal code (e.g., AZ) _____

Name for resident of this state (e.g., Californian) _____

Map It!

Research the following geographical features. Then mark each item on the blank map of the state.

- The state's major rivers and bodies of water
- The state's mountain ranges
- The highest point in the state and its elevation
- The state's capital city
- The state's five largest cities
- The state's geographical regions
- National parks in the state
- Any other special geographical features (e.g., Washington's volcanic Mount Saint Helens)
- Bordering states, nations (if Canada, specify province), and bodies of water

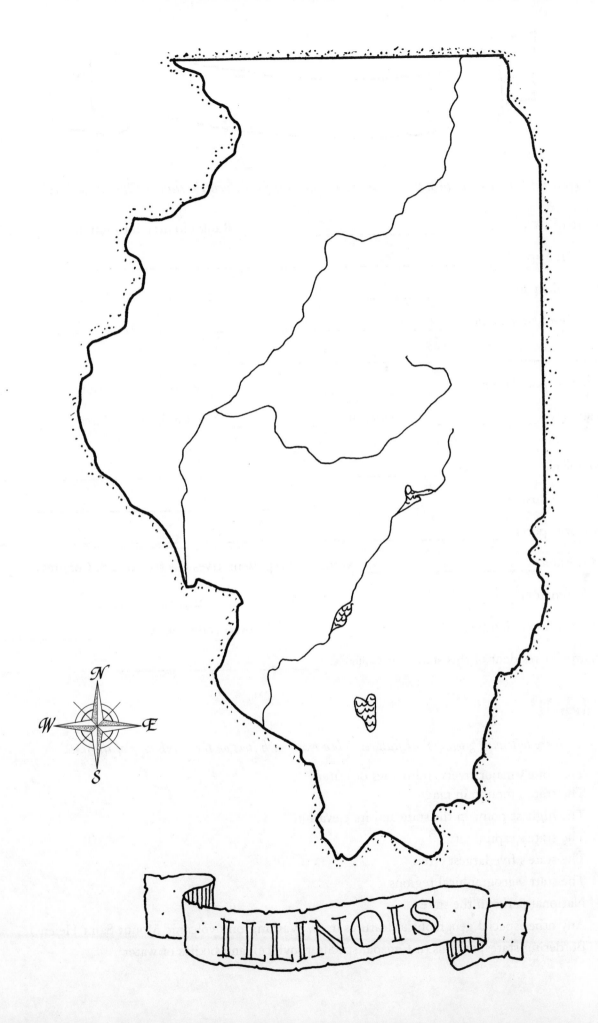

Decorate the banner with the state's name and gather these facts about the state, filling in the blanks.

Date of statehood _____ Rank of entry into union _____ of 50

State motto _____

State nickname _____

Origin of state name _____

_____

Current population _____ Rank in population _____ of 50

Land area _____ Water area _____ Rank in total area _____ of 50
        (square miles)   *(square miles)*

Major natural resources _____

Major industries _____

Major exports _____

Governor _____ Number of representatives elected to U.S. Congress _____

U.S. senators _____

State abbreviation (e.g., Ariz.) _____ Postal code (e.g., AZ) _____

Name for resident of this state (e.g., Californian) _____

Map It!

Research the following geographical features. Then mark each item on the blank map of the state.

- The state's major rivers and bodies of water
- The state's mountain ranges
- The highest point in the state and its elevation
- The state's capital city
- The state's five largest cities
- The state's geographical regions
- National parks in the state
- Any other special geographical features (e.g., Washington's volcanic Mount Saint Helens)
- Bordering states, nations (if Canada, specify province), and bodies of water

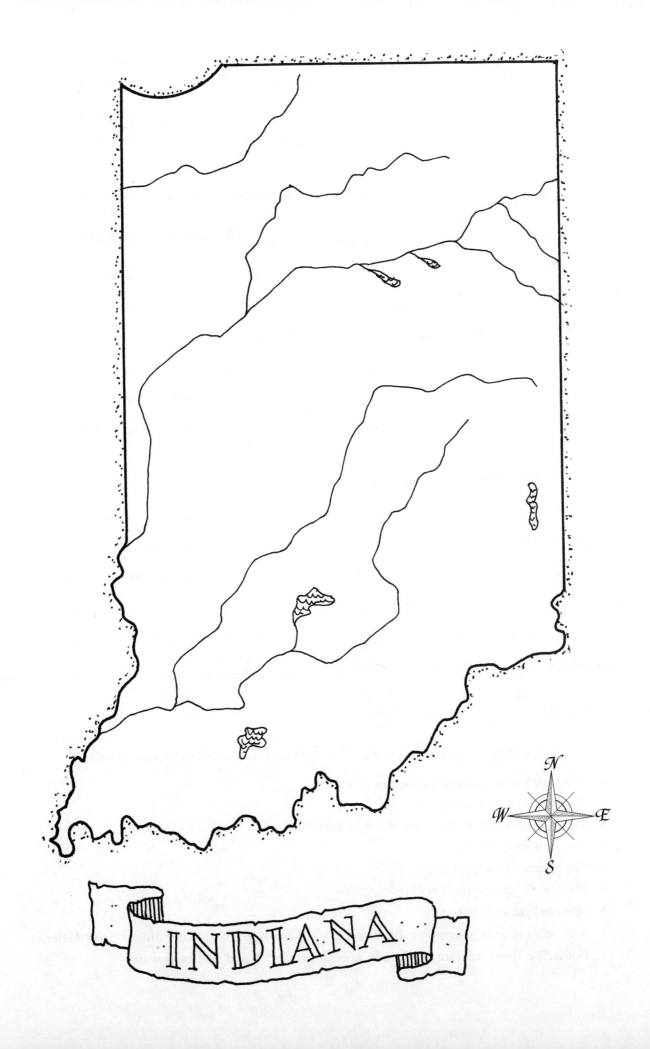

INDIANA

Decorate the banner with the state's name and gather these facts about the state, filling in the blanks.

Date of statehood _____ Rank of entry into union _____ of 50

State motto _____

State nickname _____

Origin of state name _____

_____

Current population _____ Rank in population _____ of 50

Land area _____ Water area _____ Rank in total area _____ of 50
        (square miles)   *(square miles)*

Major natural resources _____

Major industries _____

Major exports _____

Governor _____ Number of representatives elected to U.S. Congress _____

U.S. senators _____

State abbreviation (e.g., Ariz.) _____ Postal code (e.g., AZ) _____

Name for resident of this state (e.g., Californian) _____

Map It!

Research the following geographical features. Then mark each item on the blank map of the state.

- The state's major rivers and bodies of water
- The state's mountain ranges
- The highest point in the state and its elevation
- The state's capital city
- The state's five largest cities
- The state's geographical regions
- National parks in the state
- Any other special geographical features (e.g., Washington's volcanic Mount Saint Helens)
- Bordering states, nations (if Canada, specify province), and bodies of water

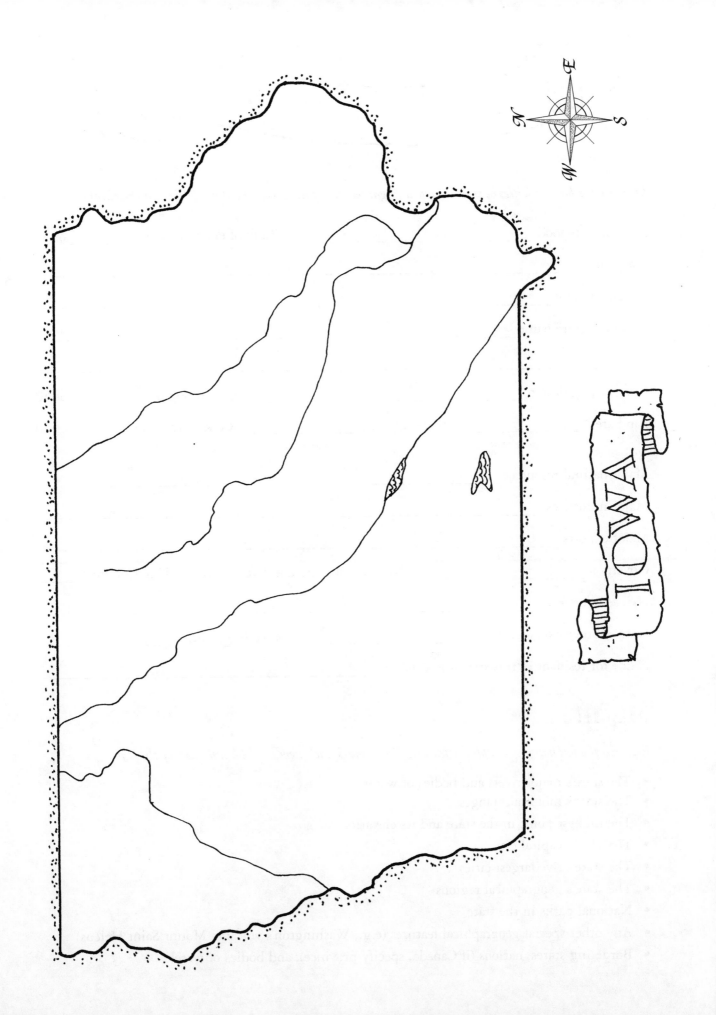

Decorate the banner with the state's name and gather these facts about the state, filling in the blanks.

Date of statehood _____ Rank of entry into union _____ of 50

State motto _____

State nickname _____

Origin of state name _____

_____

Current population _____ Rank in population _____ of 50

Land area _____ Water area _____ Rank in total area _____ of 50
    (square miles)   *(square miles)*

Major natural resources _____

Major industries _____

Major exports _____

Governor _____ Number of representatives elected to U.S. Congress _____

U.S. senators _____

State abbreviation (e.g., Ariz.) _____ Postal code (e.g., AZ) _____

Name for resident of this state (e.g., Californian) _____

Map It!

Research the following geographical features. Then mark each item on the blank map of the state.

- The state's major rivers and bodies of water
- The state's mountain ranges
- The highest point in the state and its elevation
- The state's capital city
- The state's five largest cities
- The state's geographical regions
- National parks in the state
- Any other special geographical features (e.g., Washington's volcanic Mount Saint Helens)
- Bordering states, nations (if Canada, specify province), and bodies of water

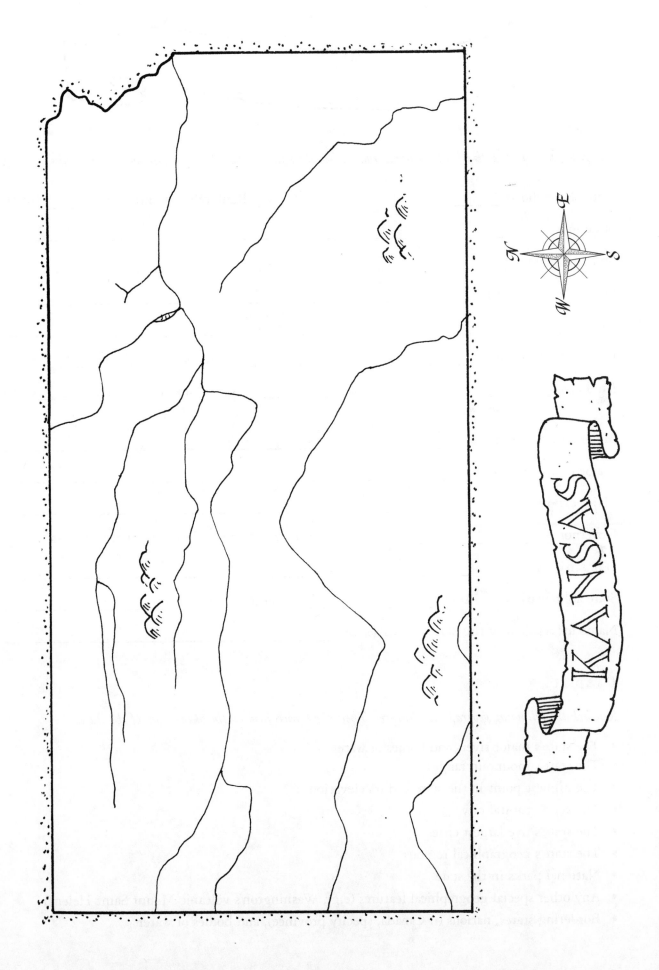

Decorate the banner with the state's name and gather these facts about the state, filling in the blanks.

Date of statehood _____ Rank of entry into union _____ of 50

State motto _____

State nickname _____

Origin of state name _____

_____

Current population _____ Rank in population _____ of 50

Land area _____ Water area _____ Rank in total area _____ of 50
                    (square miles)   *(square miles)*

Major natural resources _____

Major industries _____

Major exports _____

Governor _____ Number of representatives elected to U.S. Congress _____

U.S. senators _____

State abbreviation (e.g., Ariz.) _____ Postal code (e.g., AZ) _____

Name for resident of this state (e.g., Californian) _____

Map It!

Research the following geographical features. Then mark each item on the blank map of the state.

- The state's major rivers and bodies of water
- The state's mountain ranges
- The highest point in the state and its elevation
- The state's capital city
- The state's five largest cities
- The state's geographical regions
- National parks in the state
- Any other special geographical features (e.g., Washington's volcanic Mount Saint Helens)
- Bordering states, nations (if Canada, specify province), and bodies of water

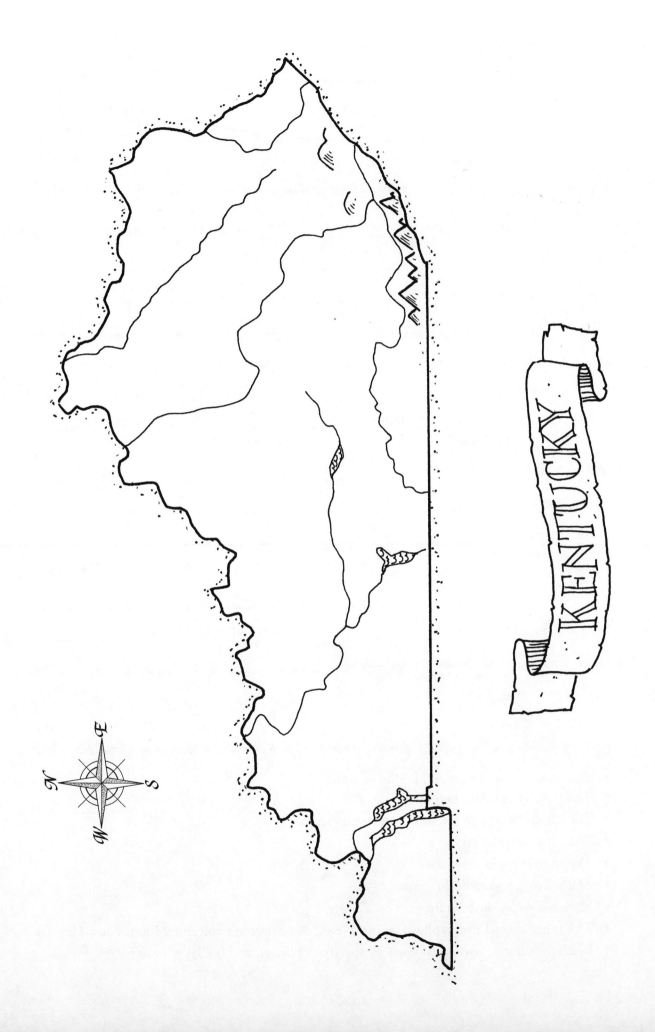

Decorate the banner with the state's name and gather these facts about the state, filling in the blanks.

Date of statehood _____ Rank of entry into union _____ of 50

State motto _____

State nickname _____

Origin of state name _____

_____

Current population _____ Rank in population _____ of 50

Land area _____ Water area _____ Rank in total area _____ of 50
       (square miles)   *(square miles)*

Major natural resources _____

Major industries _____

Major exports _____

Governor _____ Number of representatives elected to U.S. Congress _____

U.S. senators _____

State abbreviation (e.g., Ariz.) _____ Postal code (e.g., AZ) _____

Name for resident of this state (e.g., Californian) _____

Map It!

Research the following geographical features. Then mark each item on the blank map of the state.

- The state's major rivers and bodies of water
- The state's mountain ranges
- The highest point in the state and its elevation
- The state's capital city
- The state's five largest cities
- The state's geographical regions
- National parks in the state
- Any other special geographical features (e.g., Washington's volcanic Mount Saint Helens)
- Bordering states, nations (if Canada, specify province), and bodies of water

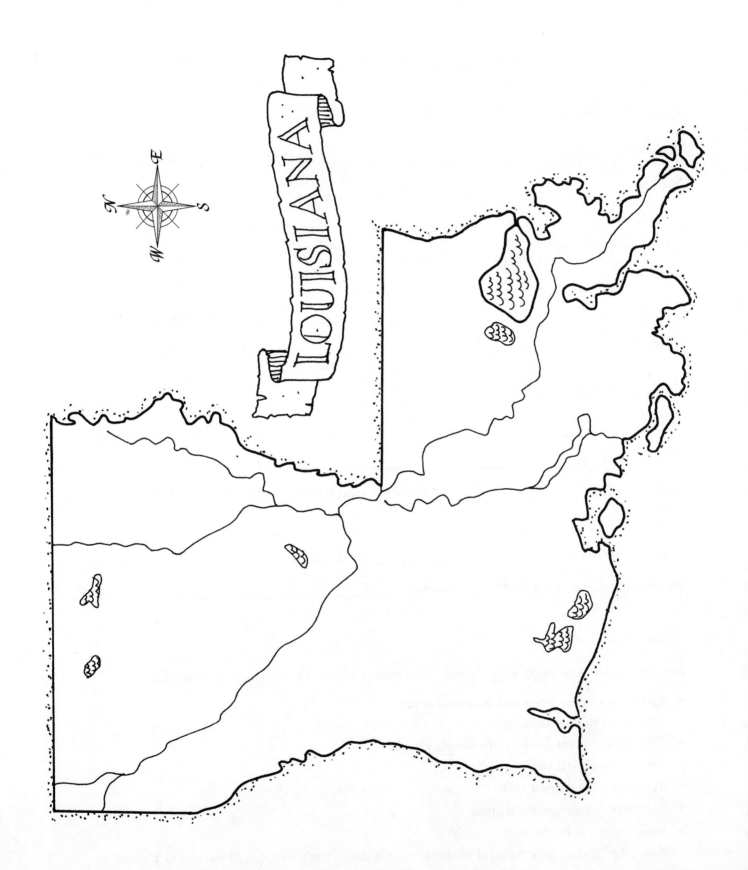

Decorate the banner with the state's name and gather these facts about the state, filling in the blanks.

Date of statehood _____ Rank of entry into union _____ of 50

State motto _____

State nickname _____

Origin of state name _____

_____

Current population _____ Rank in population _____ of 50

Land area _____ Water area _____ Rank in total area _____ of 50
      (square miles)   *(square miles)*

Major natural resources _____

Major industries _____

Major exports _____

Governor _____ Number of representatives elected to U.S. Congress _____

U.S. senators _____

State abbreviation (e.g., Ariz.) _____ Postal code (e.g., AZ) _____

Name for resident of this state (e.g., Californian) _____

Map It!

Research the following geographical features. Then mark each item on the blank map of the state.

- The state's major rivers and bodies of water
- The state's mountain ranges
- The highest point in the state and its elevation
- The state's capital city
- The state's five largest cities
- The state's geographical regions
- National parks in the state
- Any other special geographical features (e.g., Washington's volcanic Mount Saint Helens)
- Bordering states, nations (if Canada, specify province), and bodies of water

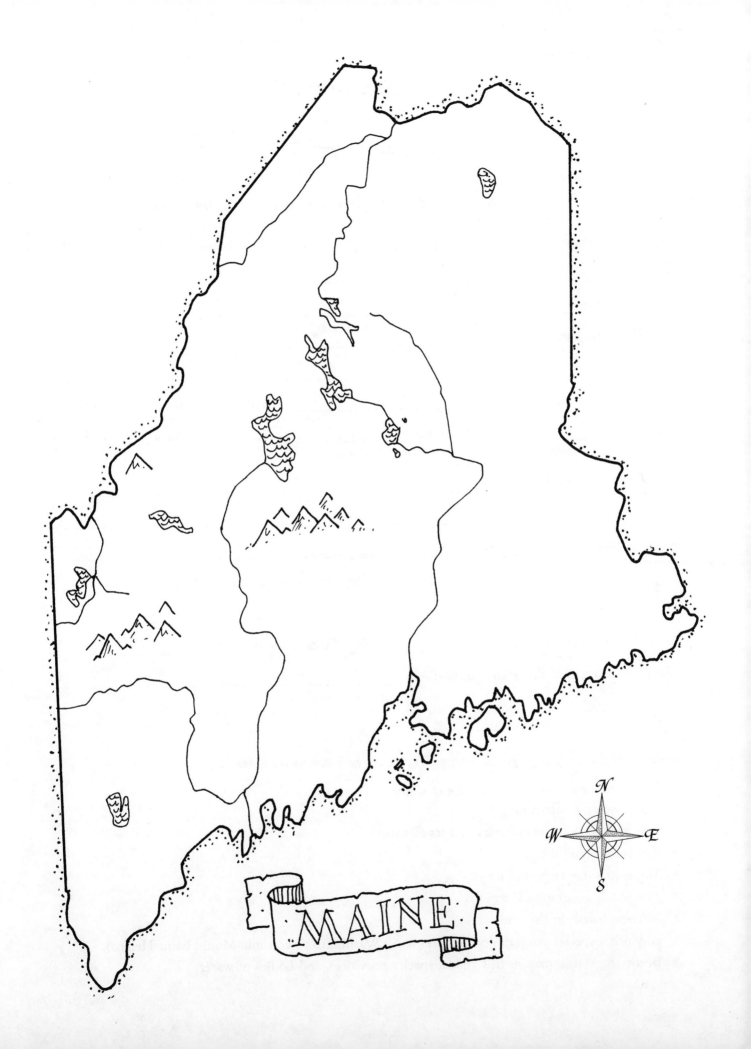

MAINE

Decorate the banner with the state's name and gather these facts about the state, filling in the blanks.

Date of statehood _____ Rank of entry into union _____ of 50

State motto _____

State nickname _____

Origin of state name _____

_____

Current population _____ Rank in population _____ of 50

Land area _____ Water area _____ Rank in total area _____ of 50
       (square miles)   *(square miles)*

Major natural resources _____

Major industries _____

Major exports _____

Governor _____ Number of representatives elected to U.S. Congress _____

U.S. senators _____

State abbreviation (e.g., Ariz.) _____ Postal code (e.g., AZ) _____

Name for resident of this state (e.g., Californian) _____

Map It!

Research the following geographical features. Then mark each item on the blank map of the state.

- The state's major rivers and bodies of water
- The state's mountain ranges
- The highest point in the state and its elevation
- The state's capital city
- The state's five largest cities
- The state's geographical regions
- National parks in the state
- Any other special geographical features (e.g., Washington's volcanic Mount Saint Helens)
- Bordering states, nations (if Canada, specify province), and bodies of water

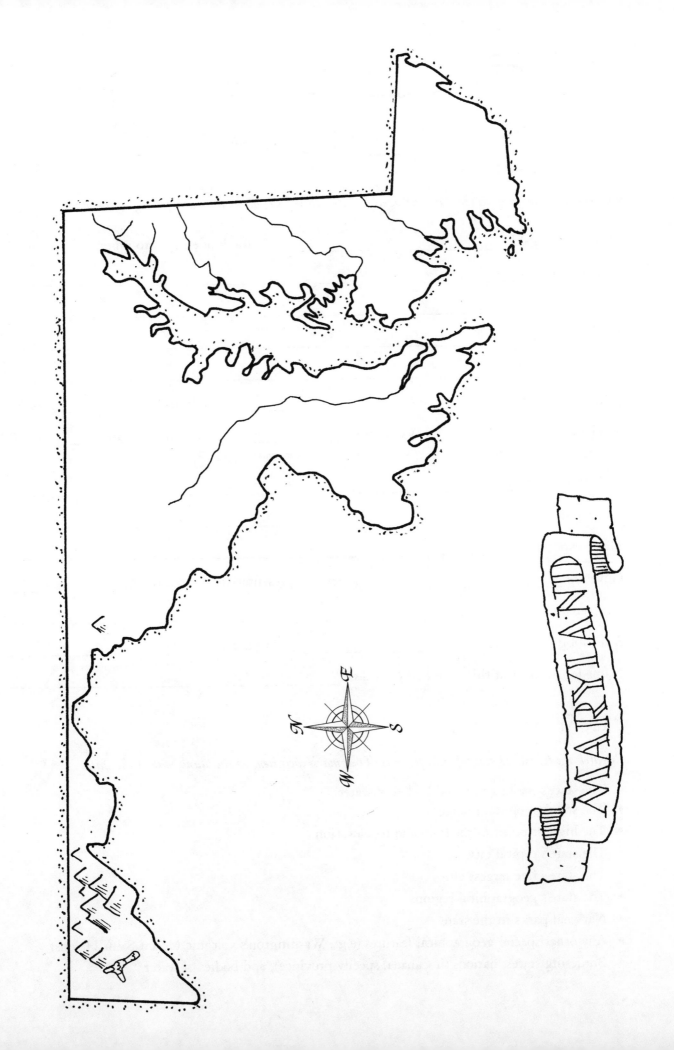

MARYLAND

Decorate the banner with the state's name and gather these facts about the state, filling in the blanks.

Date of statehood _____ Rank of entry into union _____ of 50

State motto _____

State nickname _____

Origin of state name _____

_____

Current population _____ Rank in population _____ of 50

Land area _____ Water area _____ Rank in total area _____ of 50
                (square miles)   (square miles)

Major natural resources _____

Major industries _____

Major exports _____

Governor _____ Number of representatives elected to U.S. Congress _____

U.S. senators _____

State abbreviation (e.g., Ariz.) _____ Postal code (e.g., AZ) _____

Name for resident of this state (e.g., Californian) _____

Map It!

Research the following geographical features. Then mark each item on the blank map of the state.

- The state's major rivers and bodies of water
- The state's mountain ranges
- The highest point in the state and its elevation
- The state's capital city
- The state's five largest cities
- The state's geographical regions
- National parks in the state
- Any other special geographical features (e.g., Washington's volcanic Mount Saint Helens)
- Bordering states, nations (if Canada, specify province), and bodies of water

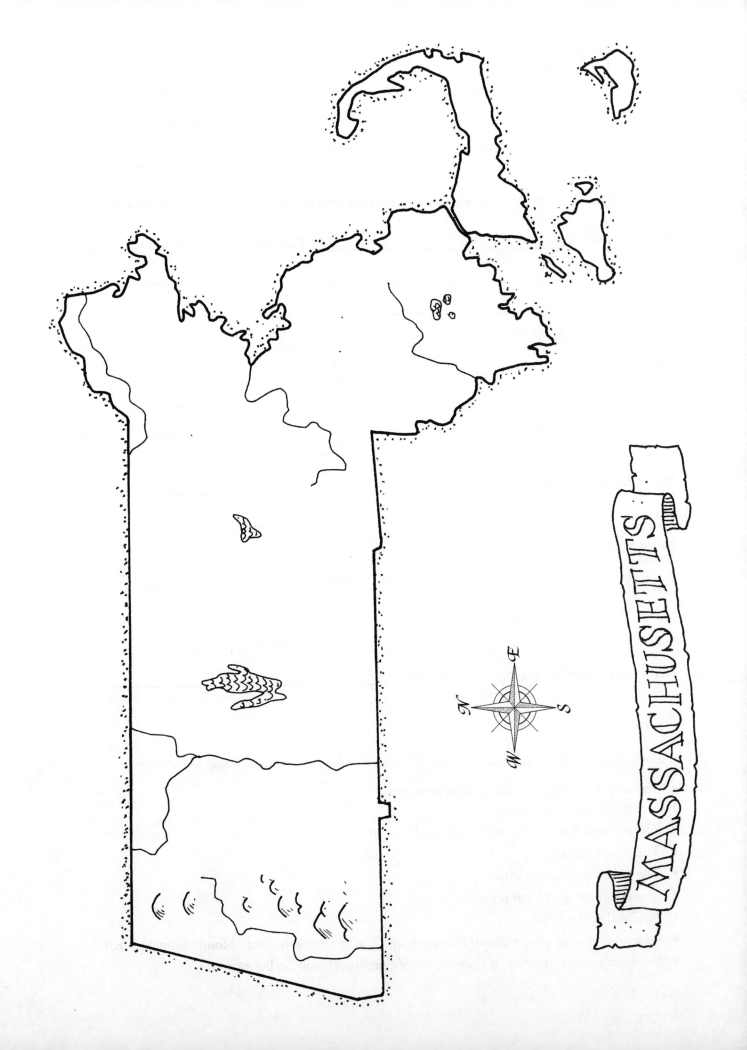

MASSACHUSETTS

Decorate the banner with the state's name and gather these facts about the state, filling in the blanks.

Date of statehood _____ Rank of entry into union _____ of 50

State motto _____

State nickname _____

Origin of state name _____

_____

Current population _____ Rank in population _____ of 50

Land area _____ Water area _____ Rank in total area _____ of 50
            (square miles)   *(square miles)*

Major natural resources _____

Major industries _____

Major exports _____

Governor _____ Number of representatives elected to U.S. Congress _____

U.S. senators _____

State abbreviation (e.g., Ariz.) _____ Postal code (e.g., AZ) _____

Name for resident of this state (e.g., Californian) _____

Map It!

Research the following geographical features. Then mark each item on the blank map of the state.

- The state's major rivers and bodies of water
- The state's mountain ranges
- The highest point in the state and its elevation
- The state's capital city
- The state's five largest cities
- The state's geographical regions
- National parks in the state
- Any other special geographical features (e.g., Washington's volcanic Mount Saint Helens)
- Bordering states, nations (if Canada, specify province), and bodies of water

MICHIGAN

Decorate the banner with the state's name and gather these facts about the state, filling in the blanks.

Date of statehood _____ Rank of entry into union _____ of 50

State motto _____

State nickname _____

Origin of state name _____

_____

Current population _____ Rank in population _____ of 50

Land area _____ Water area _____ Rank in total area _____ of 50
         (square miles)   (square miles)

Major natural resources _____

Major industries _____

Major exports _____

Governor _____ Number of representatives elected to U.S. Congress _____

U.S. senators _____

State abbreviation (e.g., Ariz.) _____ Postal code (e.g., AZ) _____

Name for resident of this state (e.g., Californian) _____

Map It!

Research the following geographical features. Then mark each item on the blank map of the state.

- The state's major rivers and bodies of water
- The state's mountain ranges
- The highest point in the state and its elevation
- The state's capital city
- The state's five largest cities
- The state's geographical regions
- National parks in the state
- Any other special geographical features (e.g., Washington's volcanic Mount Saint Helens)
- Bordering states, nations (if Canada, specify province), and bodies of water

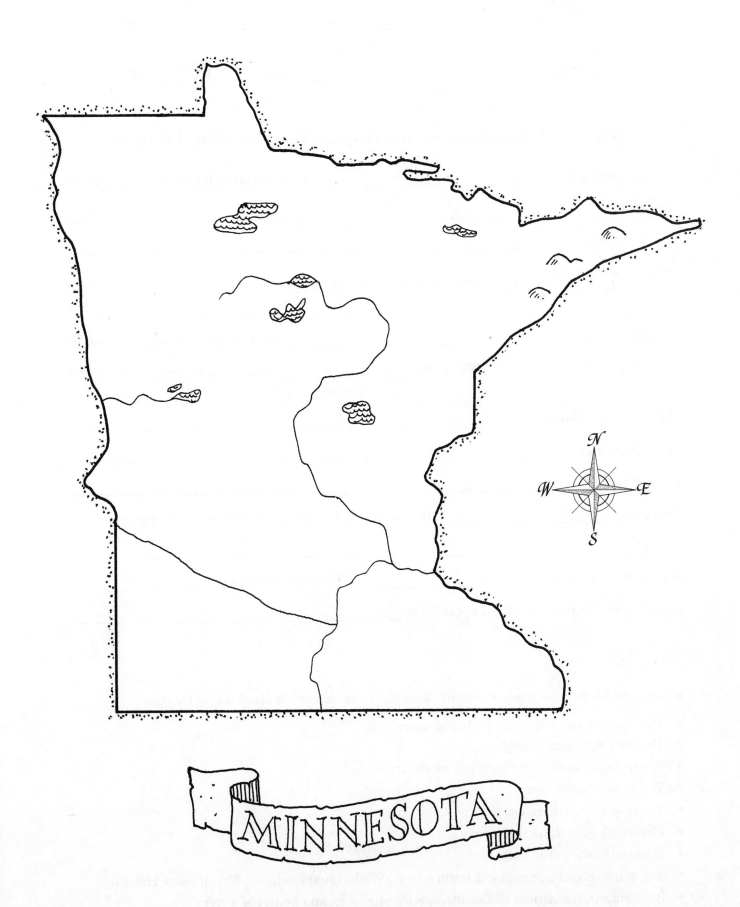

MINNESOTA

Decorate the banner with the state's name and gather these facts about the state, filling in the blanks.

Date of statehood _____ Rank of entry into union _____ of 50

State motto _____

State nickname _____

Origin of state name _____

_____

Current population _____ Rank in population _____ of 50

Land area _____ Water area _____ Rank in total area _____ of 50
      (square miles)   *(square miles)*

Major natural resources _____

Major industries _____

Major exports _____

Governor _____ Number of representatives elected to U.S. Congress _____

U.S. senators _____

State abbreviation (e.g., Ariz.) _____ Postal code (e.g., AZ) _____

Name for resident of this state (e.g., Californian) _____

Map It!

Research the following geographical features. Then mark each item on the blank map of the state.

- The state's major rivers and bodies of water
- The state's mountain ranges
- The highest point in the state and its elevation
- The state's capital city
- The state's five largest cities
- The state's geographical regions
- National parks in the state
- Any other special geographical features (e.g., Washington's volcanic Mount Saint Helens)
- Bordering states, nations (if Canada, specify province), and bodies of water

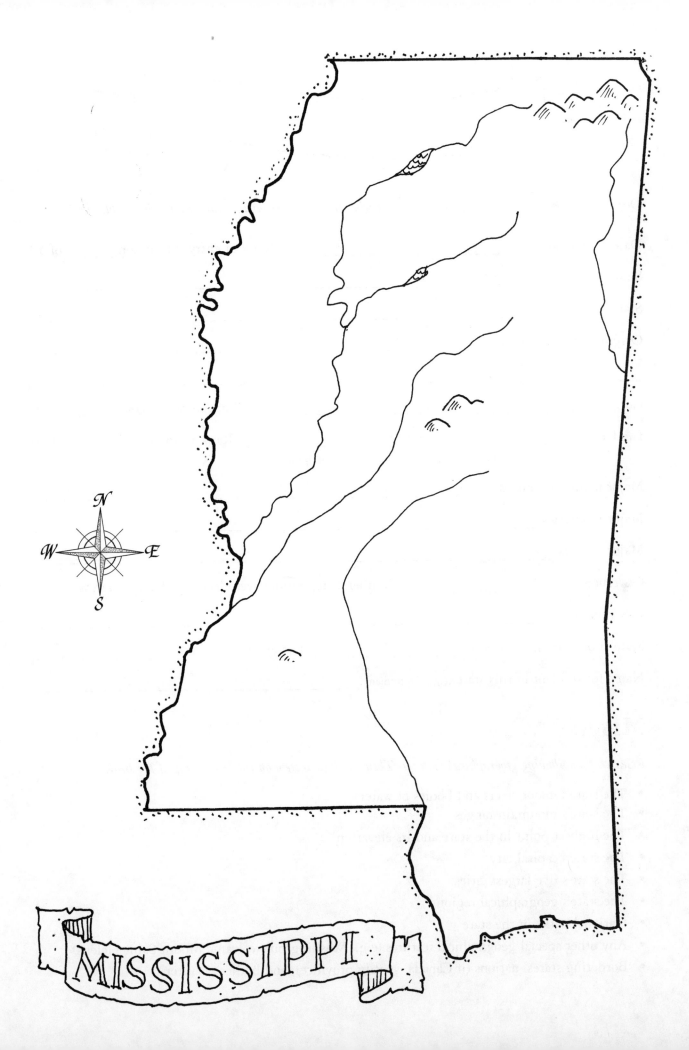

MISSISSIPPI

Decorate the banner with the state's name and gather these facts about the state, filling in the blanks.

Date of statehood _____ Rank of entry into union _____ of 50

State motto _____

State nickname _____

Origin of state name _____

_____

Current population _____ Rank in population _____ of 50

Land area _____ Water area _____ Rank in total area _____ of 50
                (square miles)   *(square miles)*

Major natural resources _____

Major industries _____

Major exports _____

Governor _____ Number of representatives elected to U.S. Congress _____

U.S. senators _____

State abbreviation (e.g., Ariz.) _____ Postal code (e.g., AZ) _____

Name for resident of this state (e.g., Californian) _____

Map It!

Research the following geographical features. Then mark each item on the blank map of the state.

- The state's major rivers and bodies of water
- The state's mountain ranges
- The highest point in the state and its elevation
- The state's capital city
- The state's five largest cities
- The state's geographical regions
- National parks in the state
- Any other special geographical features (e.g., Washington's volcanic Mount Saint Helens)
- Bordering states, nations (if Canada, specify province), and bodies of water

MISSOURI

Decorate the banner with the state's name and gather these facts about the state, filling in the blanks.

Date of statehood _____ Rank of entry into union _____ of 50

State motto _____

State nickname _____

Origin of state name _____

_____

Current population _____ Rank in population _____ of 50

Land area _____ Water area _____ Rank in total area _____ of 50
      (square miles)   *(square miles)*

Major natural resources _____

Major industries _____

Major exports _____

Governor _____ Number of representatives elected to U.S. Congress _____

U.S. senators _____

State abbreviation (e.g., Ariz.) _____ Postal code (e.g., AZ) _____

Name for resident of this state (e.g., Californian) _____

Map It!

Research the following geographical features. Then mark each item on the blank map of the state.

- The state's major rivers and bodies of water
- The state's mountain ranges
- The highest point in the state and its elevation
- The state's capital city
- The state's five largest cities
- The state's geographical regions
- National parks in the state
- Any other special geographical features (e.g., Washington's volcanic Mount Saint Helens)
- Bordering states, nations (if Canada, specify province), and bodies of water

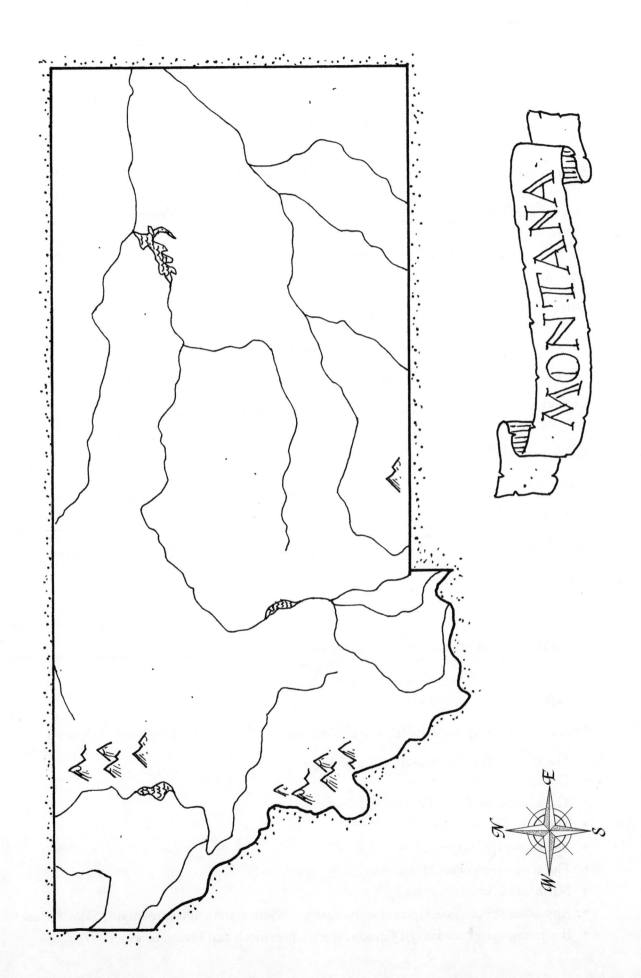

Decorate the banner with the state's name and gather these facts about the state, filling in the blanks.

Date of statehood _____ Rank of entry into union _____ of 50

State motto _____

State nickname _____

Origin of state name _____

_____

Current population _____ Rank in population _____ of 50

Land area _____ Water area _____ Rank in total area _____ of 50
        (square miles)   *(square miles)*

Major natural resources _____

Major industries _____

Major exports _____

Governor _____ Number of representatives elected to U.S. Congress _____

U.S. senators _____

State abbreviation (e.g., Ariz.) _____ Postal code (e.g., AZ) _____

Name for resident of this state (e.g., Californian) _____

Map It!

Research the following geographical features. Then mark each item on the blank map of the state.

- The state's major rivers and bodies of water
- The state's mountain ranges
- The highest point in the state and its elevation
- The state's capital city
- The state's five largest cities
- The state's geographical regions
- National parks in the state
- Any other special geographical features (e.g., Washington's volcanic Mount Saint Helens)
- Bordering states, nations (if Canada, specify province), and bodies of water

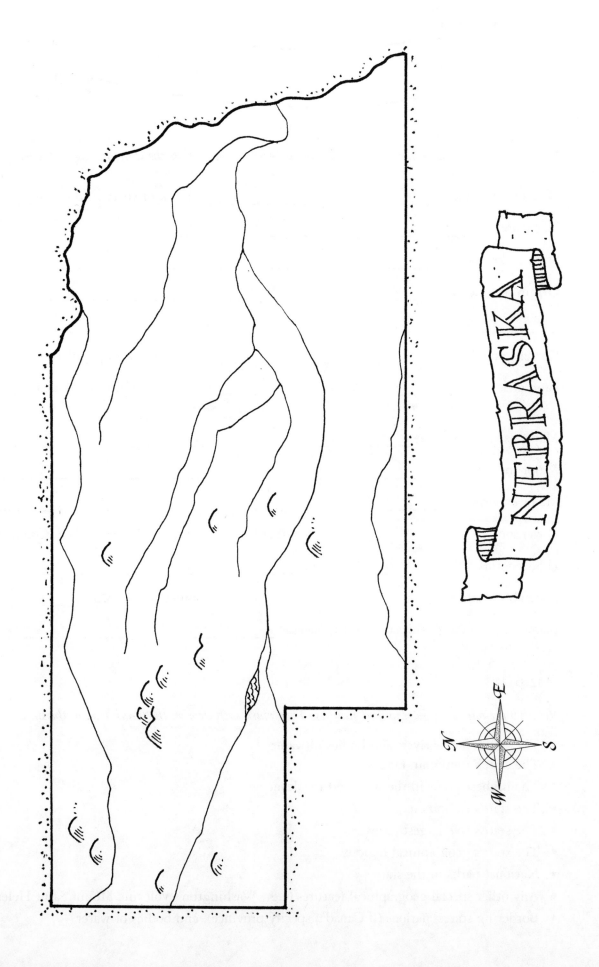

Decorate the banner with the state's name and gather these facts about the state, filling in the blanks.

Date of statehood _____ Rank of entry into union _____ of 50

State motto _____

State nickname _____

Origin of state name _____

_____

Current population _____ Rank in population _____ of 50

Land area _____ Water area _____ Rank in total area _____ of 50
      (square miles)   *(square miles)*

Major natural resources _____

Major industries _____

Major exports _____

Governor _____ Number of representatives elected to U.S. Congress _____

U.S. senators _____

State abbreviation (e.g., Ariz.) _____ Postal code (e.g., AZ) _____

Name for resident of this state (e.g., Californian) _____

Map It!

Research the following geographical features. Then mark each item on the blank map of the state.

- The state's major rivers and bodies of water
- The state's mountain ranges
- The highest point in the state and its elevation
- The state's capital city
- The state's five largest cities
- The state's geographical regions
- National parks in the state
- Any other special geographical features (e.g., Washington's volcanic Mount Saint Helens)
- Bordering states, nations (if Canada, specify province), and bodies of water

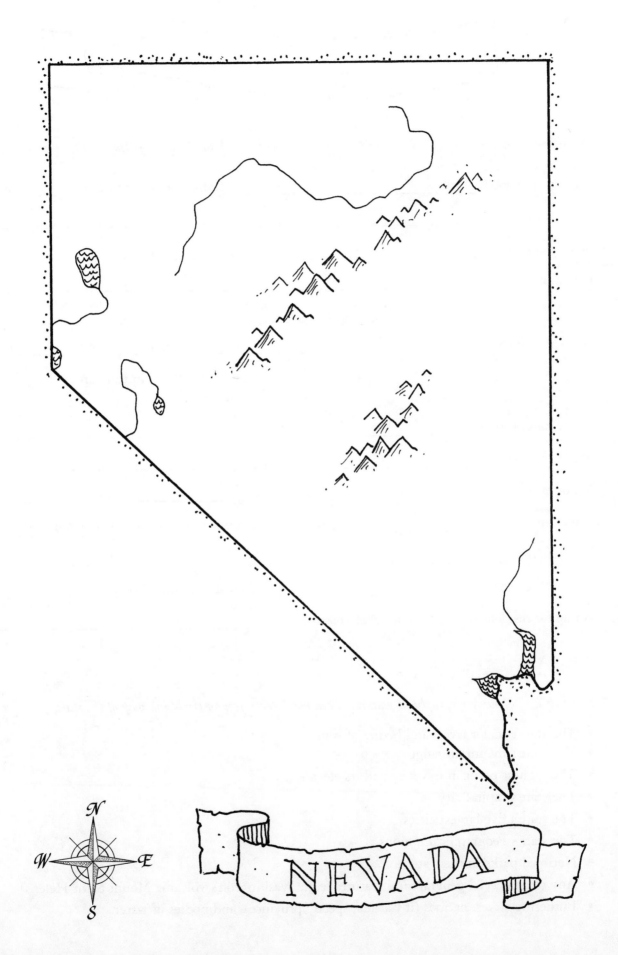

NEVADA

Decorate the banner with the state's name and gather these facts about the state, filling in the blanks.

Date of statehood _____ Rank of entry into union _____ of 50

State motto _____

State nickname _____

Origin of state name _____

_____

Current population _____ Rank in population _____ of 50

Land area _____ Water area _____ Rank in total area _____ of 50

        (square miles)   *(square miles)*

Major natural resources _____

Major industries _____

Major exports _____

Governor _____ Number of representatives elected to U.S. Congress _____

U.S. senators _____

State abbreviation (e.g., Ariz.) _____ Postal code (e.g., AZ) _____

Name for resident of this state (e.g., Californian) _____

Map It!

Research the following geographical features. Then mark each item on the blank map of the state.

- The state's major rivers and bodies of water
- The state's mountain ranges
- The highest point in the state and its elevation
- The state's capital city
- The state's five largest cities
- The state's geographical regions
- National parks in the state
- Any other special geographical features (e.g., Washington's volcanic Mount Saint Helens)
- Bordering states, nations (if Canada, specify province), and bodies of water

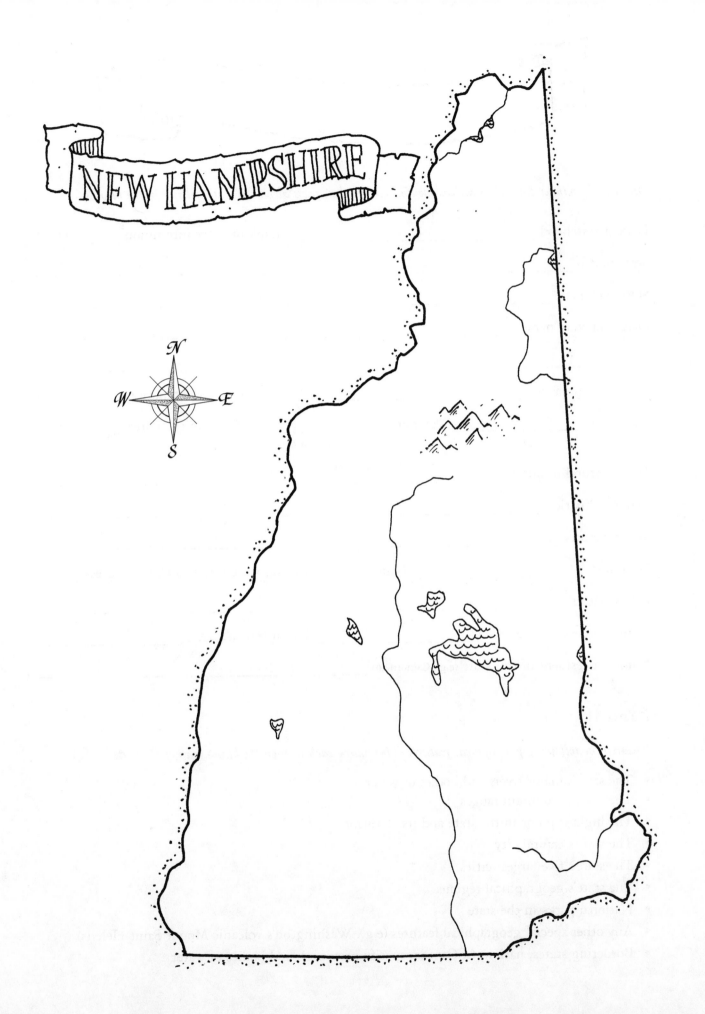

Decorate the banner with the state's name and gather these facts about the state, filling in the blanks.

Date of statehood _____ Rank of entry into union _____ of 50

State motto _____

State nickname _____

Origin of state name _____

_____

Current population _____ Rank in population _____ of 50

Land area _____ Water area _____ Rank in total area _____ of 50
            (square miles)   *(square miles)*

Major natural resources _____

Major industries _____

Major exports _____

Governor _____ Number of representatives elected to U.S. Congress _____

U.S. senators _____

State abbreviation (e.g., Ariz.) _____ Postal code (e.g., AZ) _____

Name for resident of this state (e.g., Californian) _____

Map It!

Research the following geographical features. Then mark each item on the blank map of the state.

- The state's major rivers and bodies of water
- The state's mountain ranges
- The highest point in the state and its elevation
- The state's capital city
- The state's five largest cities
- The state's geographical regions
- National parks in the state
- Any other special geographical features (e.g., Washington's volcanic Mount Saint Helens)
- Bordering states, nations (if Canada, specify province), and bodies of water

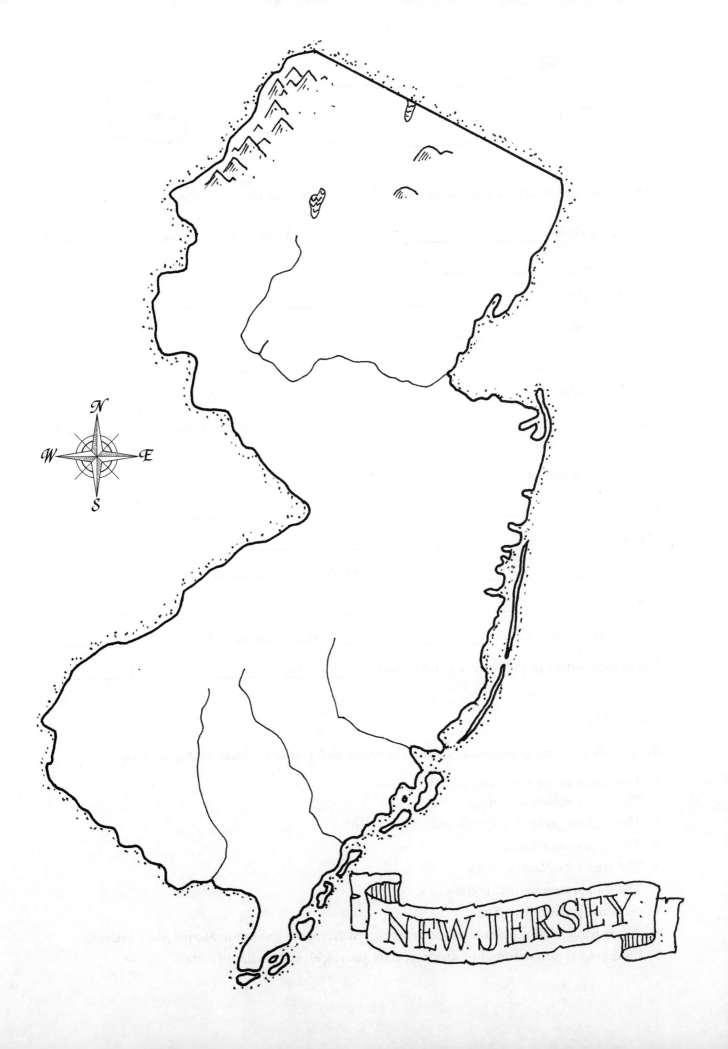

Decorate the banner with the state's name and gather these facts about the state, filling in the blanks.

Date of statehood _____ Rank of entry into union _____ of 50

State motto _____

State nickname _____

Origin of state name _____

_____

Current population _____ Rank in population _____ of 50

Land area _____ Water area _____ Rank in total area _____ of 50
        (square miles)   *(square miles)*

Major natural resources _____

Major industries _____

Major exports _____

Governor _____ Number of representatives elected to U.S. Congress _____

U.S. senators _____

State abbreviation (e.g., Ariz.) _____ Postal code (e.g., AZ) _____

Name for resident of this state (e.g., Californian) _____

Map It!

Research the following geographical features. Then mark each item on the blank map of the state.

- The state's major rivers and bodies of water
- The state's mountain ranges
- The highest point in the state and its elevation
- The state's capital city
- The state's five largest cities
- The state's geographical regions
- National parks in the state
- Any other special geographical features (e.g., Washington's volcanic Mount Saint Helens)
- Bordering states, nations (if Canada, specify province), and bodies of water

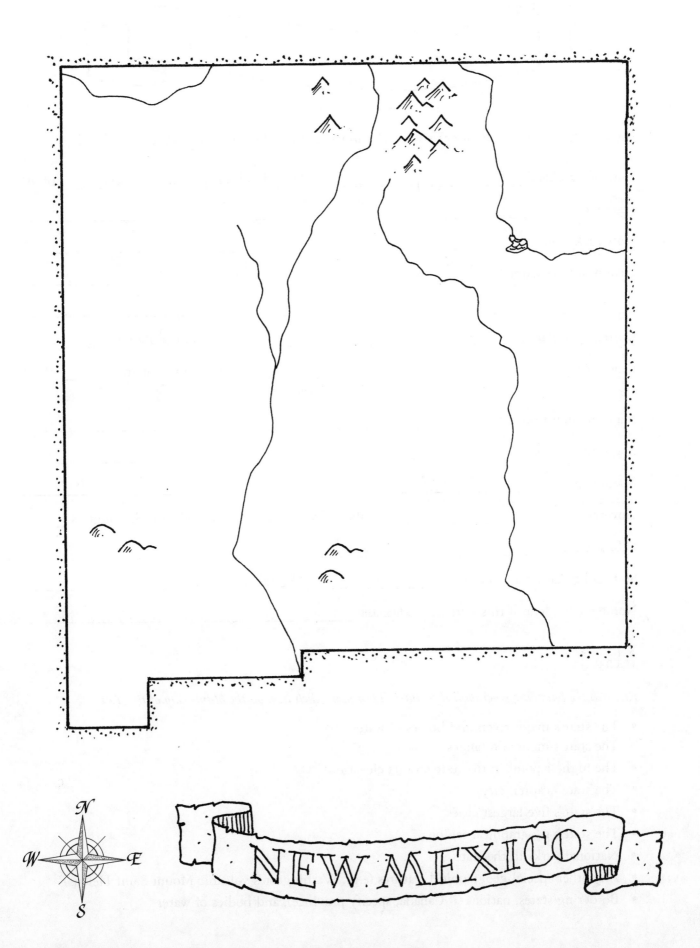

NEW MEXICO

Decorate the banner with the state's name and gather these facts about the state, filling in the blanks.

Date of statehood _____ Rank of entry into union _____ of 50

State motto _____

State nickname _____

Origin of state name _____

_____

Current population _____ Rank in population _____ of 50

Land area _____ Water area _____ Rank in total area _____ of 50
　　　　　　　(square miles)　　　　　　　　　　*(square miles)*

Major natural resources _____

Major industries _____

Major exports _____

Governor _____ Number of representatives elected to U.S. Congress _____

U.S. senators _____

State abbreviation (e.g., Ariz.) _____ Postal code (e.g., AZ) _____

Name for resident of this state (e.g., Californian) _____

Map It!

Research the following geographical features. Then mark each item on the blank map of the state.

- The state's major rivers and bodies of water
- The state's mountain ranges
- The highest point in the state and its elevation
- The state's capital city
- The state's five largest cities
- The state's geographical regions
- National parks in the state
- Any other special geographical features (e.g., Washington's volcanic Mount Saint Helens)
- Bordering states, nations (if Canada, specify province), and bodies of water

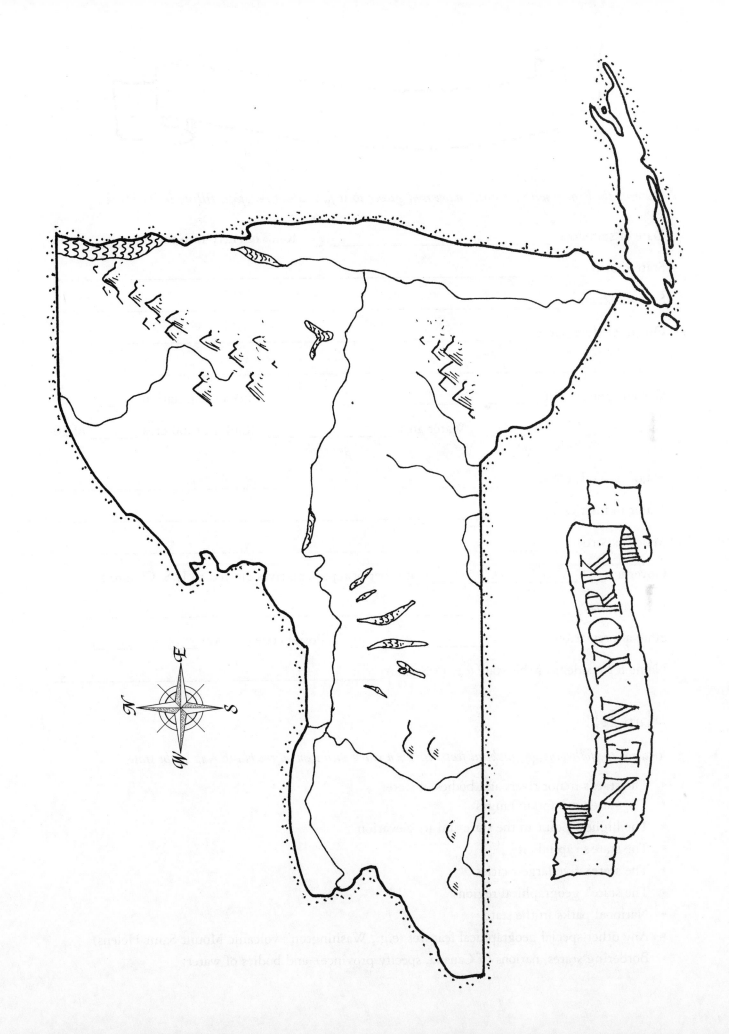

Decorate the banner with the state's name and gather these facts about the state, filling in the blanks.

Date of statehood _____ Rank of entry into union _____ of 50

State motto _____

State nickname _____

Origin of state name _____

_____

Current population _____ Rank in population _____ of 50

Land area _____ Water area _____ Rank in total area _____ of 50
　　　　　(square miles)　　　　　　　　　*(square miles)*

Major natural resources _____

Major industries _____

Major exports _____

Governor _____ Number of representatives elected to U.S. Congress _____

U.S. senators _____

State abbreviation (e.g., Ariz.) _____ Postal code (e.g., AZ) _____

Name for resident of this state (e.g., Californian) _____

Map It!

Research the following geographical features. Then mark each item on the blank map of the state.

- The state's major rivers and bodies of water
- The state's mountain ranges
- The highest point in the state and its elevation
- The state's capital city
- The state's five largest cities
- The state's geographical regions
- National parks in the state
- Any other special geographical features (e.g., Washington's volcanic Mount Saint Helens)
- Bordering states, nations (if Canada, specify province), and bodies of water

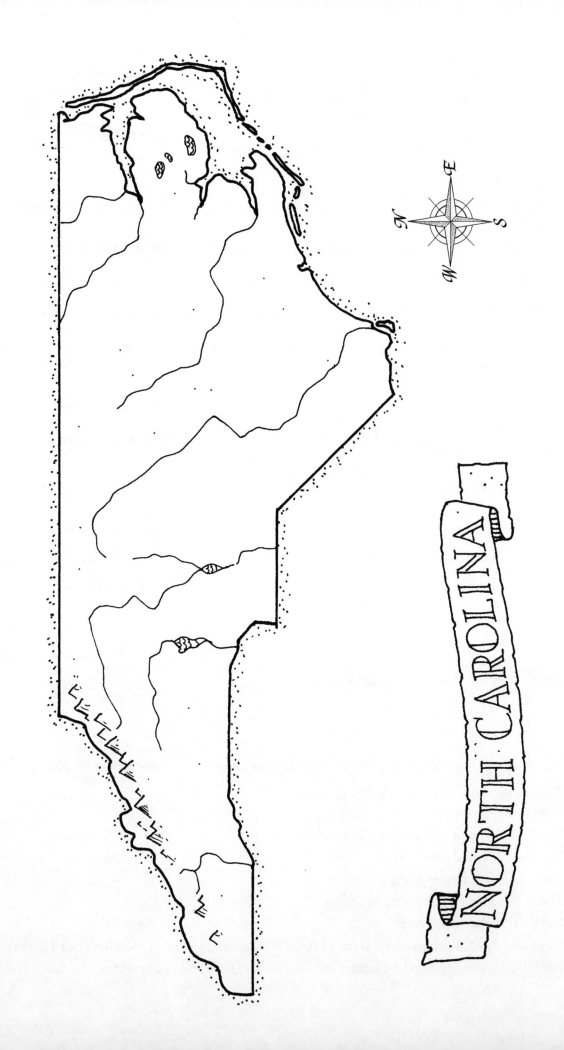

Decorate the banner with the state's name and gather these facts about the state, filling in the blanks.

Date of statehood _____ Rank of entry into union _____ of 50

State motto _____

State nickname _____

Origin of state name _____

_____

Current population _____ Rank in population _____ of 50

Land area _____ Water area _____ Rank in total area _____ of 50
        (square miles)   *(square miles)*

Major natural resources _____

Major industries _____

Major exports _____

Governor _____ Number of representatives elected to U.S. Congress _____

U.S. senators _____

State abbreviation (e.g., Ariz.) _____ Postal code (e.g., AZ) _____

Name for resident of this state (e.g., Californian) _____

Map It!

Research the following geographical features. Then mark each item on the blank map of the state.

- The state's major rivers and bodies of water
- The state's mountain ranges
- The highest point in the state and its elevation
- The state's capital city
- The state's five largest cities
- The state's geographical regions
- National parks in the state
- Any other special geographical features (e.g., Washington's volcanic Mount Saint Helens)
- Bordering states, nations (if Canada, specify province), and bodies of water

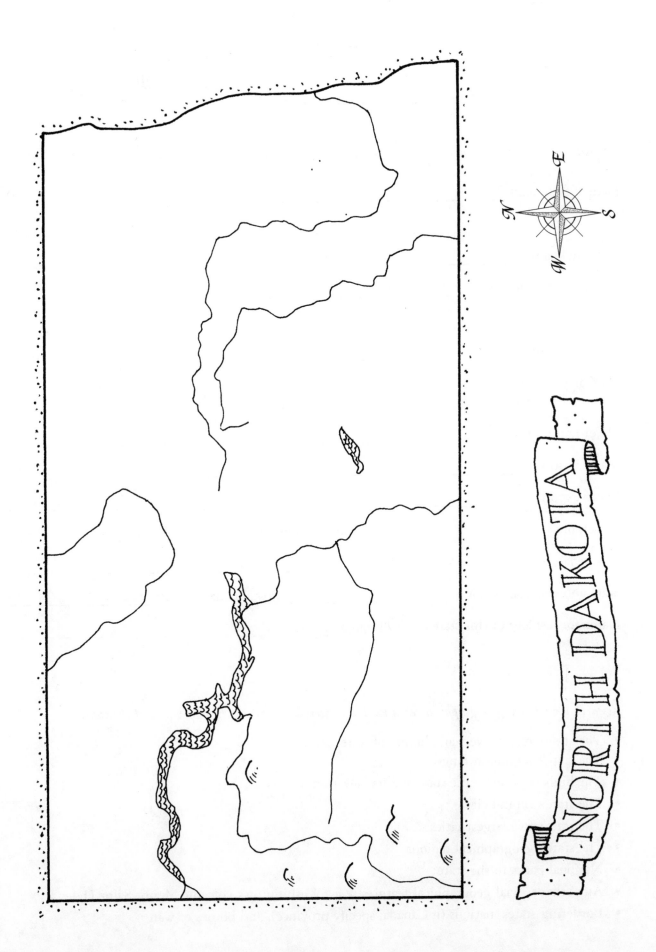

NORTH DAKOTA

Decorate the banner with the state's name and gather these facts about the state, filling in the blanks.

Date of statehood _____ Rank of entry into union _____ of 50

State motto _____

State nickname _____

Origin of state name _____

_____

Current population _____ Rank in population _____ of 50

Land area _____ Water area _____ Rank in total area _____ of 50
　　　　　　(square miles)　　　　　　　　　　*(square miles)*

Major natural resources _____

Major industries _____

Major exports _____

Governor _____ Number of representatives elected to U.S. Congress _____

U.S. senators _____

State abbreviation (e.g., Ariz.) _____ Postal code (e.g., AZ) _____

Name for resident of this state (e.g., Californian) _____

Map It!

Research the following geographical features. Then mark each item on the blank map of the state.

- The state's major rivers and bodies of water
- The state's mountain ranges
- The highest point in the state and its elevation
- The state's capital city
- The state's five largest cities
- The state's geographical regions
- National parks in the state
- Any other special geographical features (e.g., Washington's volcanic Mount Saint Helens)
- Bordering states, nations (if Canada, specify province), and bodies of water

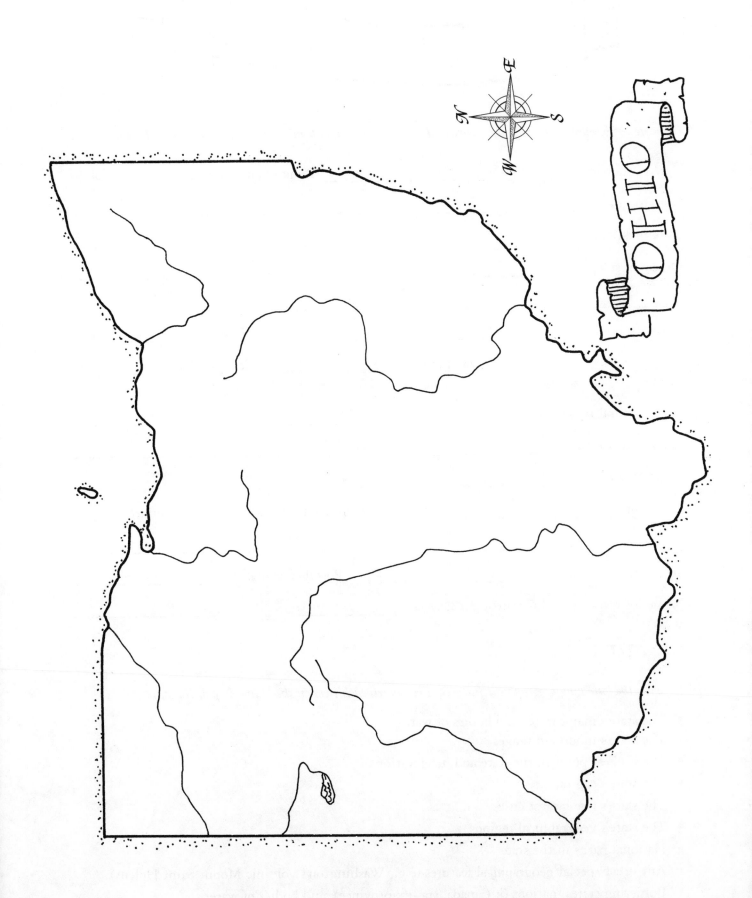

Decorate the banner with the state's name and gather these facts about the state, filling in the blanks.

Date of statehood _____ Rank of entry into union _____ of 50

State motto _____

State nickname _____

Origin of state name _____

_____

Current population _____ Rank in population _____ of 50

Land area _____ Water area _____ Rank in total area _____ of 50
　　　　　(square miles)　　　　　　　　　　　(square miles)

Major natural resources _____

Major industries _____

Major exports _____

Governor _____ Number of representatives elected to U.S. Congress _____

U.S. senators _____

State abbreviation (e.g., Ariz.) _____ Postal code (e.g., AZ) _____

Name for resident of this state (e.g., Californian) _____

Map It!

Research the following geographical features. Then mark each item on the blank map of the state.

- The state's major rivers and bodies of water
- The state's mountain ranges
- The highest point in the state and its elevation
- The state's capital city
- The state's five largest cities
- The state's geographical regions
- National parks in the state
- Any other special geographical features (e.g., Washington's volcanic Mount Saint Helens)
- Bordering states, nations (if Canada, specify province), and bodies of water

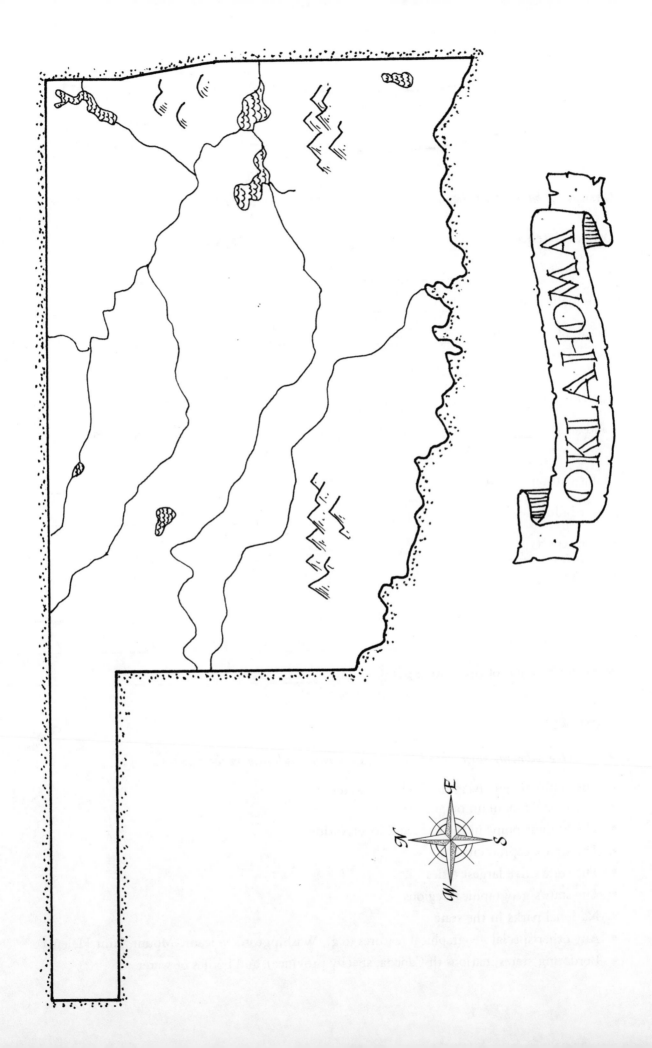

Decorate the banner with the state's name and gather these facts about the state, filling in the blanks.

Date of statehood _____ Rank of entry into union _____ of 50

State motto _____

State nickname _____

Origin of state name _____

_____

Current population _____ Rank in population _____ of 50

Land area _____ Water area _____ Rank in total area _____ of 50
      (square miles)   *(square miles)*

Major natural resources _____

Major industries _____

Major exports _____

Governor _____ Number of representatives elected to U.S. Congress _____

U.S. senators _____

State abbreviation (e.g., Ariz.) _____ Postal code (e.g., AZ) _____

Name for resident of this state (e.g., Californian) _____

Map It!

Research the following geographical features. Then mark each item on the blank map of the state.

- The state's major rivers and bodies of water
- The state's mountain ranges
- The highest point in the state and its elevation
- The state's capital city
- The state's five largest cities
- The state's geographical regions
- National parks in the state
- Any other special geographical features (e.g., Washington's volcanic Mount Saint Helens)
- Bordering states, nations (if Canada, specify province), and bodies of water

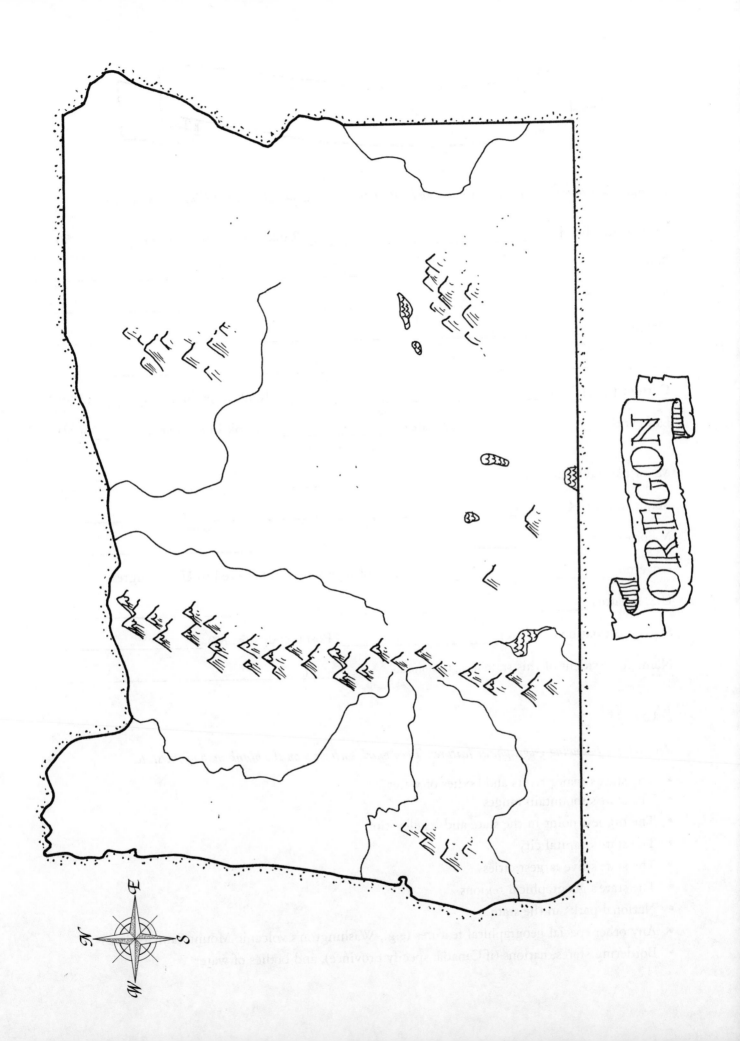

Decorate the banner with the state's name and gather these facts about the state, filling in the blanks.

Date of statehood _____ Rank of entry into union _____ of 50

State motto _____

State nickname _____

Origin of state name _____

_____

Current population _____ Rank in population _____ of 50

Land area _____ Water area _____ Rank in total area _____ of 50
      (square miles)   *(square miles)*

Major natural resources _____

Major industries _____

Major exports _____

Governor _____ Number of representatives elected to U.S. Congress _____

U.S. senators _____

State abbreviation (e.g., Ariz.) _____ Postal code (e.g., AZ) _____

Name for resident of this state (e.g., Californian) _____

Map It!

Research the following geographical features. Then mark each item on the blank map of the state.

- The state's major rivers and bodies of water
- The state's mountain ranges
- The highest point in the state and its elevation
- The state's capital city
- The state's five largest cities
- The state's geographical regions
- National parks in the state
- Any other special geographical features (e.g., Washington's volcanic Mount Saint Helens)
- Bordering states, nations (if Canada, specify province), and bodies of water

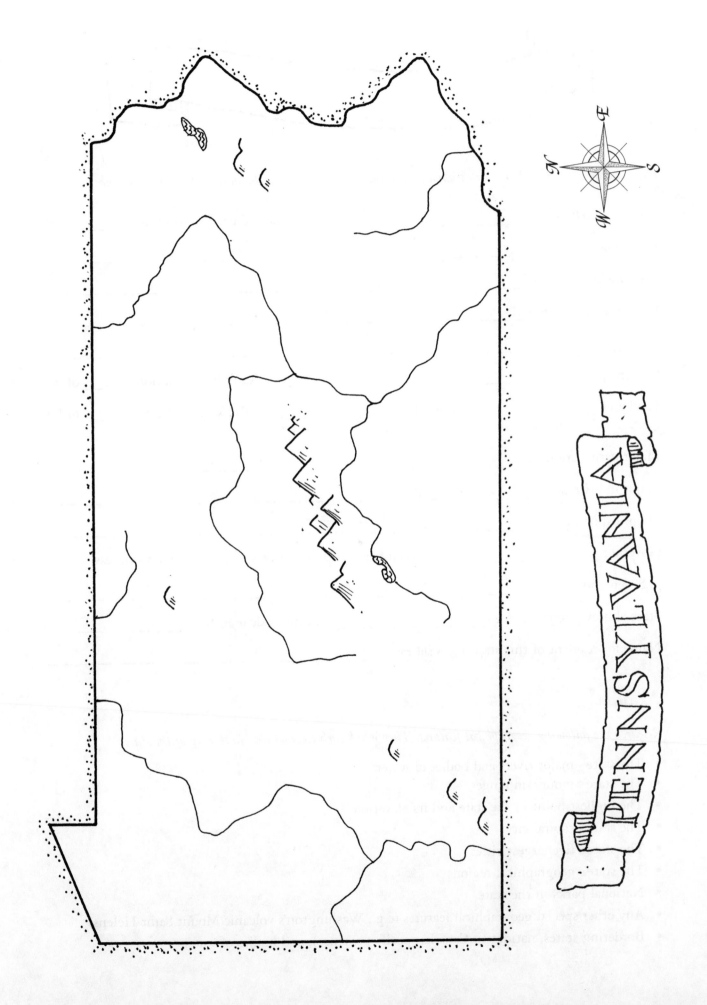

Decorate the banner with the state's name and gather these facts about the state, filling in the blanks.

Date of statehood _____ Rank of entry into union _____ of 50

State motto _____

State nickname _____

Origin of state name _____

_____

Current population _____ Rank in population _____ of 50

Land area _____ Water area _____ Rank in total area _____ of 50
(square miles) *(square miles)*

Major natural resources _____

Major industries _____

Major exports _____

Governor _____ Number of representatives elected to U.S. Congress _____

U.S. senators _____

State abbreviation (e.g., Ariz.) _____ Postal code (e.g., AZ) _____

Name for resident of this state (e.g., Californian) _____

Map It!

Research the following geographical features. Then mark each item on the blank map of the state.

- The state's major rivers and bodies of water
- The state's mountain ranges
- The highest point in the state and its elevation
- The state's capital city
- The state's five largest cities
- The state's geographical regions
- National parks in the state
- Any other special geographical features (e.g., Washington's volcanic Mount Saint Helens)
- Bordering states, nations (if Canada, specify province), and bodies of water

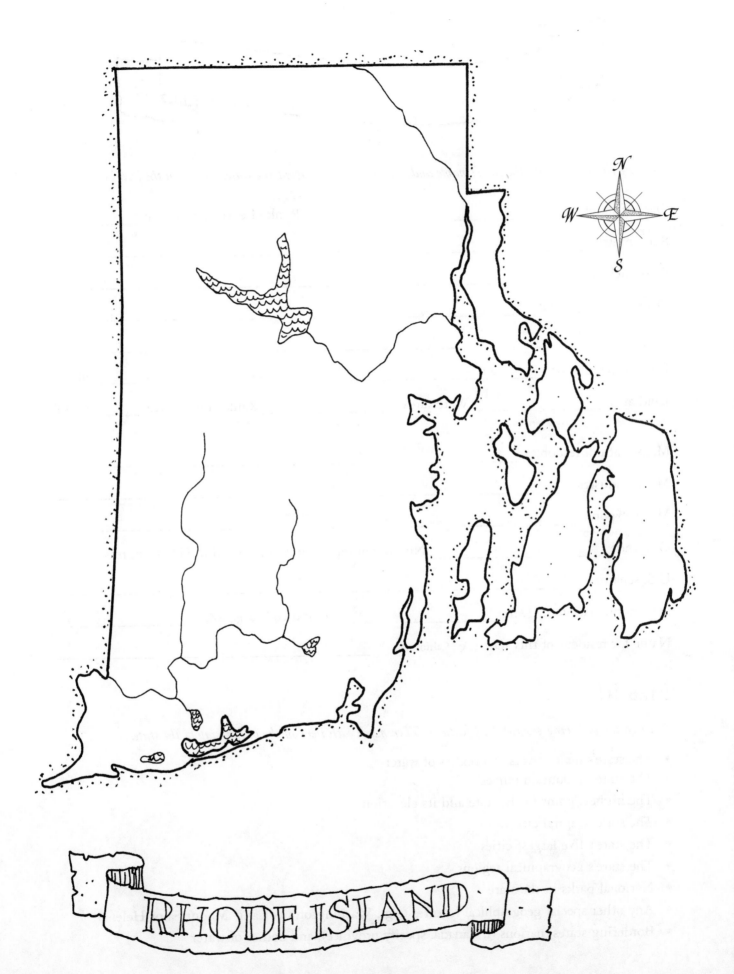

RHODE ISLAND

Decorate the banner with the state's name and gather these facts about the state, filling in the blanks.

Date of statehood _____ Rank of entry into union _____ of 50

State motto _____

State nickname _____

Origin of state name _____

_____

Current population _____ Rank in population _____ of 50

Land area _____ Water area _____ Rank in total area _____ of 50
      (square miles)   *(square miles)*

Major natural resources _____

Major industries _____

Major exports _____

Governor _____ Number of representatives elected to U.S. Congress _____

U.S. senators _____

State abbreviation (e.g., Ariz.) _____ Postal code (e.g., AZ) _____

Name for resident of this state (e.g., Californian) _____

Map It!

Research the following geographical features. Then mark each item on the blank map of the state.

- The state's major rivers and bodies of water
- The state's mountain ranges
- The highest point in the state and its elevation
- The state's capital city
- The state's five largest cities
- The state's geographical regions
- National parks in the state
- Any other special geographical features (e.g., Washington's volcanic Mount Saint Helens)
- Bordering states, nations (if Canada, specify province), and bodies of water

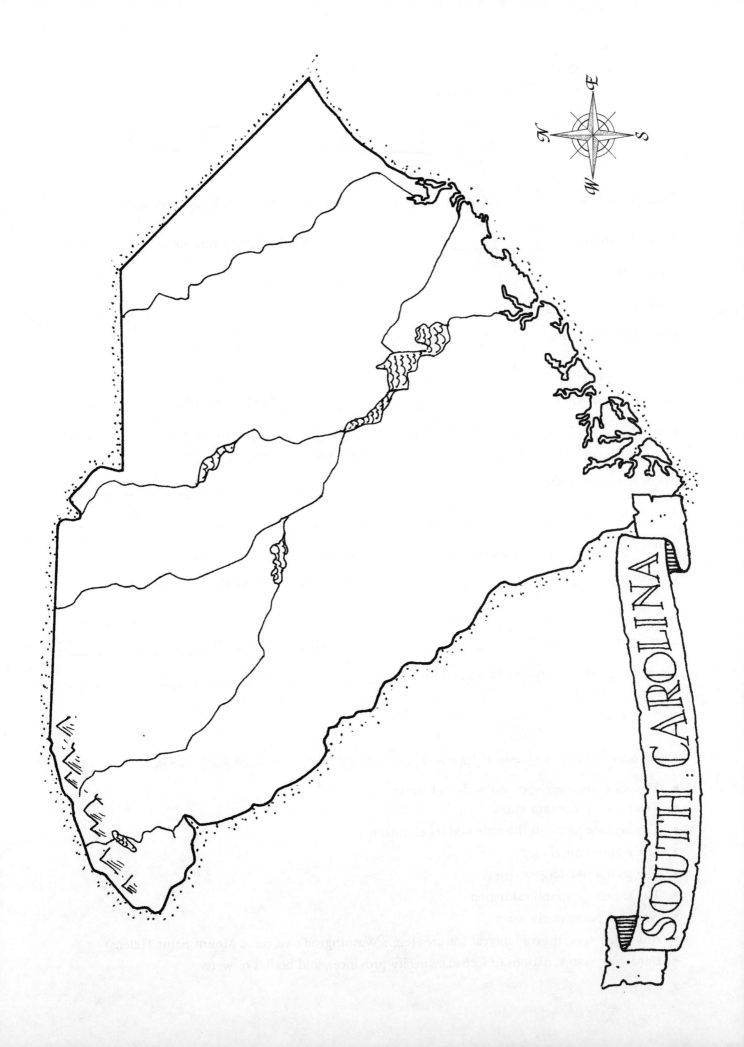

SOUTH CAROLINA

Decorate the banner with the state's name and gather these facts about the state, filling in the blanks.

Date of statehood _____ Rank of entry into union _____ of 50

State motto _____

State nickname _____

Origin of state name _____

_____

Current population _____ Rank in population _____ of 50

Land area _____ Water area _____ Rank in total area _____ of 50
       (square miles)   *(square miles)*

Major natural resources _____

Major industries _____

Major exports _____

Governor _____ Number of representatives elected to U.S. Congress _____

U.S. senators _____

State abbreviation (e.g., Ariz.) _____ Postal code (e.g., AZ) _____

Name for resident of this state (e.g., Californian) _____

Map It!

Research the following geographical features. Then mark each item on the blank map of the state.

- The state's major rivers and bodies of water
- The state's mountain ranges
- The highest point in the state and its elevation
- The state's capital city
- The state's five largest cities
- The state's geographical regions
- National parks in the state
- Any other special geographical features (e.g., Washington's volcanic Mount Saint Helens)
- Bordering states, nations (if Canada, specify province), and bodies of water

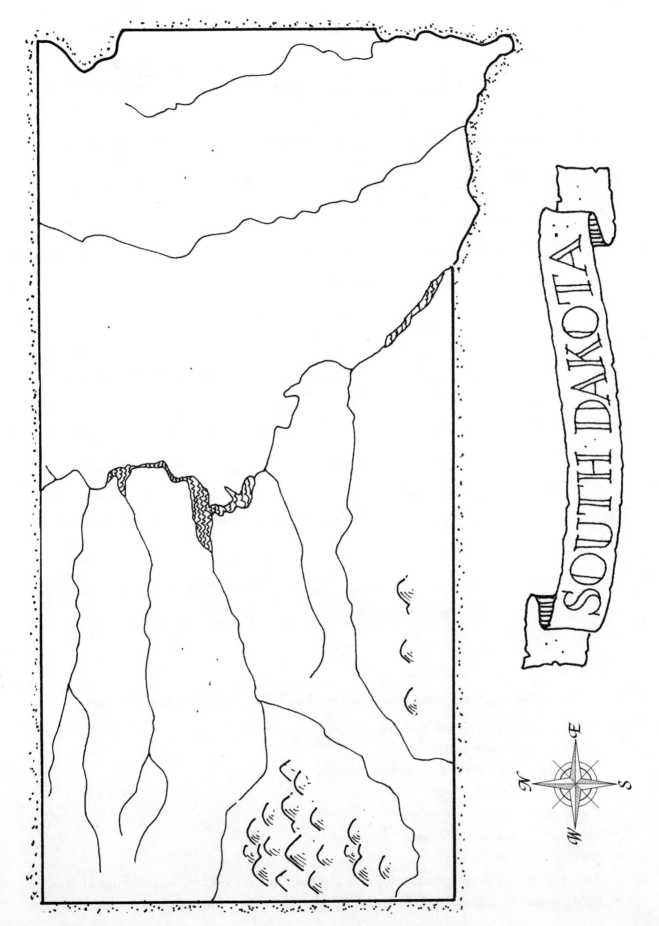

SOUTH DAKOTA

Decorate the banner with the state's name and gather these facts about the state, filling in the blanks.

Date of statehood _____ Rank of entry into union _____ of 50

State motto _____

State nickname _____

Origin of state name _____

_____

Current population _____ Rank in population _____ of 50

Land area _____ Water area _____ Rank in total area _____ of 50
         (square miles)   *(square miles)*

Major natural resources _____

Major industries _____

Major exports _____

Governor _____ Number of representatives elected to U.S. Congress _____

U.S. senators _____

State abbreviation (e.g., Ariz.) _____ Postal code (e.g., AZ) _____

Name for resident of this state (e.g., Californian) _____

Map It!

Research the following geographical features. Then mark each item on the blank map of the state.

- The state's major rivers and bodies of water
- The state's mountain ranges
- The highest point in the state and its elevation
- The state's capital city
- The state's five largest cities
- The state's geographical regions
- National parks in the state
- Any other special geographical features (e.g., Washington's volcanic Mount Saint Helens)
- Bordering states, nations (if Canada, specify province), and bodies of water

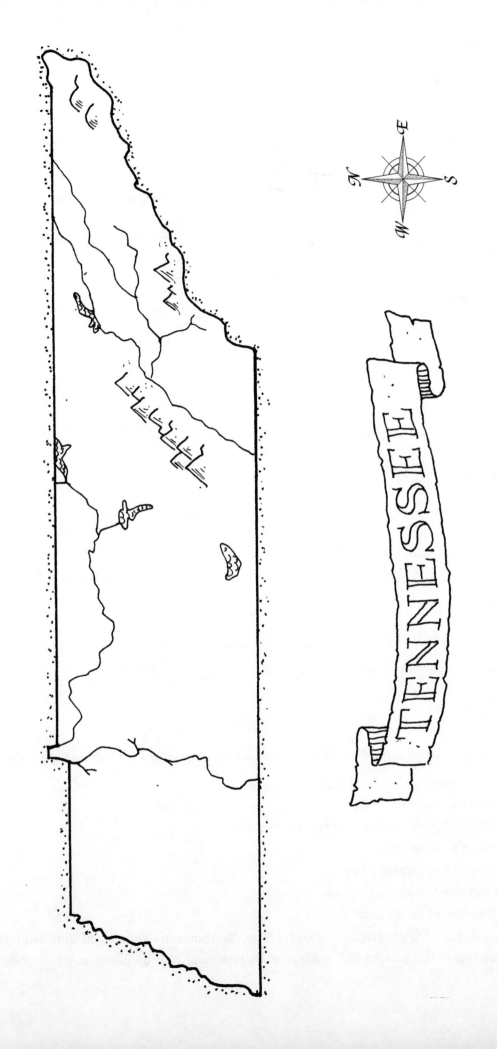

Decorate the banner with the state's name and gather these facts about the state, filling in the blanks.

Date of statehood _____ Rank of entry into union _____ of 50

State motto _____

State nickname _____

Origin of state name _____

_____

Current population _____ Rank in population _____ of 50

Land area _____ Water area _____ Rank in total area _____ of 50
            (square miles)   *(square miles)*

Major natural resources _____

Major industries _____

Major exports _____

Governor _____ Number of representatives elected to U.S. Congress _____

U.S. senators _____

State abbreviation (e.g., Ariz.) _____ Postal code (e.g., AZ) _____

Name for resident of this state (e.g., Californian) _____

Map It!

Research the following geographical features. Then mark each item on the blank map of the state.

- The state's major rivers and bodies of water
- The state's mountain ranges
- The highest point in the state and its elevation
- The state's capital city
- The state's five largest cities
- The state's geographical regions
- National parks in the state
- Any other special geographical features (e.g., Washington's volcanic Mount Saint Helens)
- Bordering states, nations (if Canada, specify province), and bodies of water

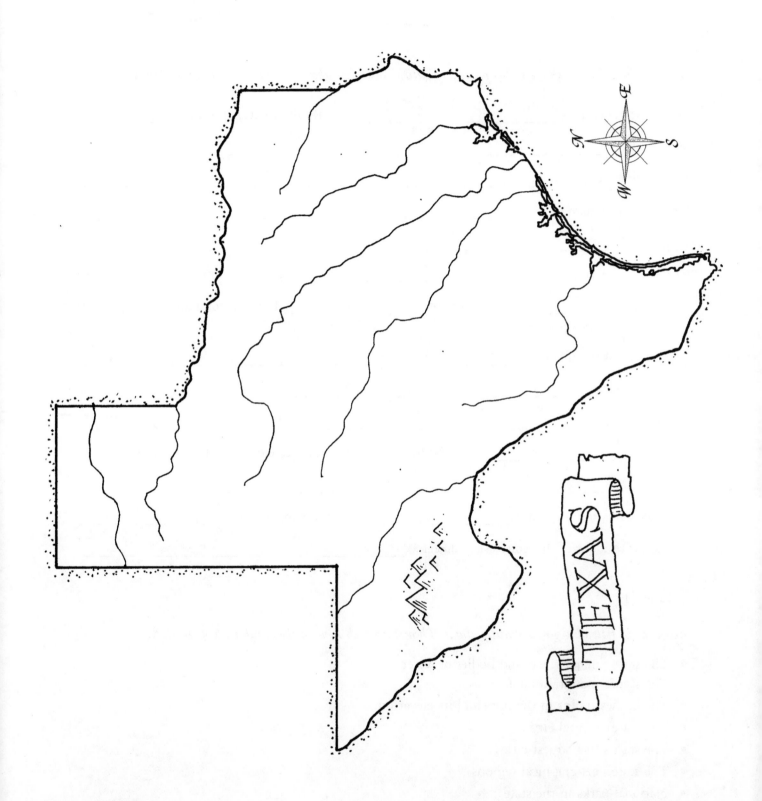

Decorate the banner with the state's name and gather these facts about the state, filling in the blanks.

Date of statehood _____ Rank of entry into union _____ of 50

State motto _____

State nickname _____

Origin of state name _____

_____

Current population _____ Rank in population _____ of 50

Land area _____ Water area _____ Rank in total area _____ of 50
       (square miles)   *(square miles)*

Major natural resources _____

Major industries _____

Major exports _____

Governor _____ Number of representatives elected to U.S. Congress _____

U.S. senators _____

State abbreviation (e.g., Ariz.) _____ Postal code (e.g., AZ) _____

Name for resident of this state (e.g., Californian) _____

Map It!

Research the following geographical features. Then mark each item on the blank map of the state.

- The state's major rivers and bodies of water
- The state's mountain ranges
- The highest point in the state and its elevation
- The state's capital city
- The state's five largest cities
- The state's geographical regions
- National parks in the state
- Any other special geographical features (e.g., Washington's volcanic Mount Saint Helens)
- Bordering states, nations (if Canada, specify province), and bodies of water

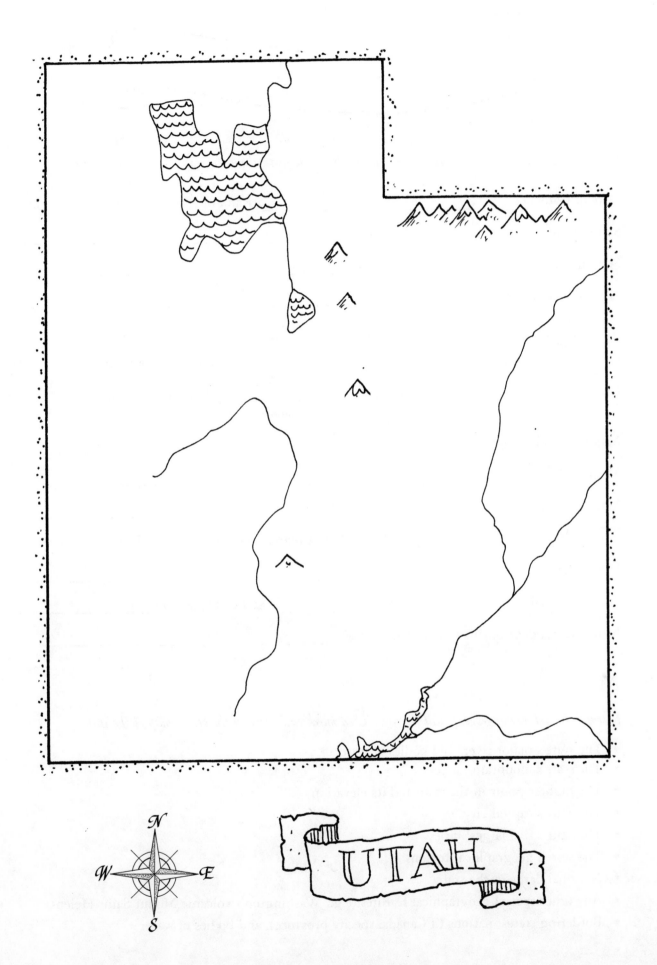

UTAH

Decorate the banner with the state's name and gather these facts about the state, filling in the blanks.

Date of statehood _____ Rank of entry into union _____ of 50

State motto _____

State nickname _____

Origin of state name _____

_____

Current population _____ Rank in population _____ of 50

Land area _____ Water area _____ Rank in total area _____ of 50
      (square miles)   *(square miles)*

Major natural resources _____

Major industries _____

Major exports _____

Governor _____ Number of representatives elected to U.S. Congress _____

U.S. senators _____

State abbreviation (e.g., Ariz.) _____ Postal code (e.g., AZ) _____

Name for resident of this state (e.g., Californian) _____

Map It!

Research the following geographical features. Then mark each item on the blank map of the state.

- The state's major rivers and bodies of water
- The state's mountain ranges
- The highest point in the state and its elevation
- The state's capital city
- The state's five largest cities
- The state's geographical regions
- National parks in the state
- Any other special geographical features (e.g., Washington's volcanic Mount Saint Helens)
- Bordering states, nations (if Canada, specify province), and bodies of water

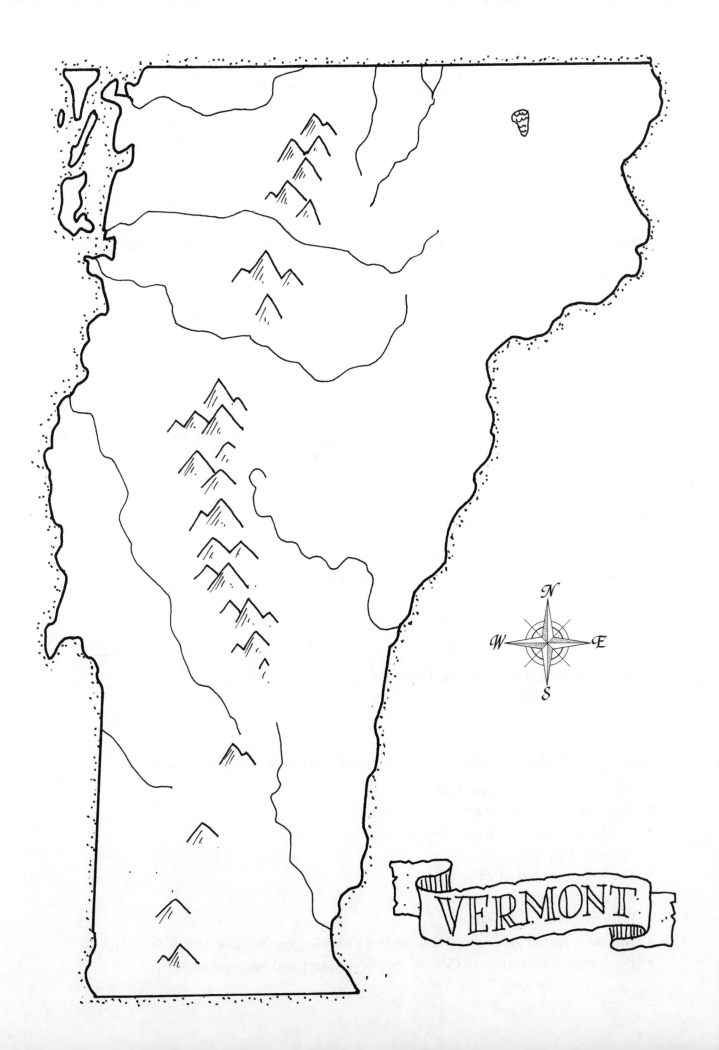

VERMONT

Decorate the banner with the state's name and gather these facts about the state, filling in the blanks.

Date of statehood _____ Rank of entry into union _____ of 50

State motto _____

State nickname _____

Origin of state name _____

_____

Current population _____ Rank in population _____ of 50

Land area _____ Water area _____ Rank in total area _____ of 50
　　　　　(square miles)　　　　　　　　　　*(square miles)*

Major natural resources _____

Major industries _____

Major exports _____

Governor _____ Number of representatives elected to U.S. Congress _____

U.S. senators _____

State abbreviation (e.g., Ariz.) _____ Postal code (e.g., AZ) _____

Name for resident of this state (e.g., Californian) _____

Map It!

Research the following geographical features. Then mark each item on the blank map of the state.

- The state's major rivers and bodies of water
- The state's mountain ranges
- The highest point in the state and its elevation
- The state's capital city
- The state's five largest cities
- The state's geographical regions
- National parks in the state
- Any other special geographical features (e.g., Washington's volcanic Mount Saint Helens)
- Bordering states, nations (if Canada, specify province), and bodies of water

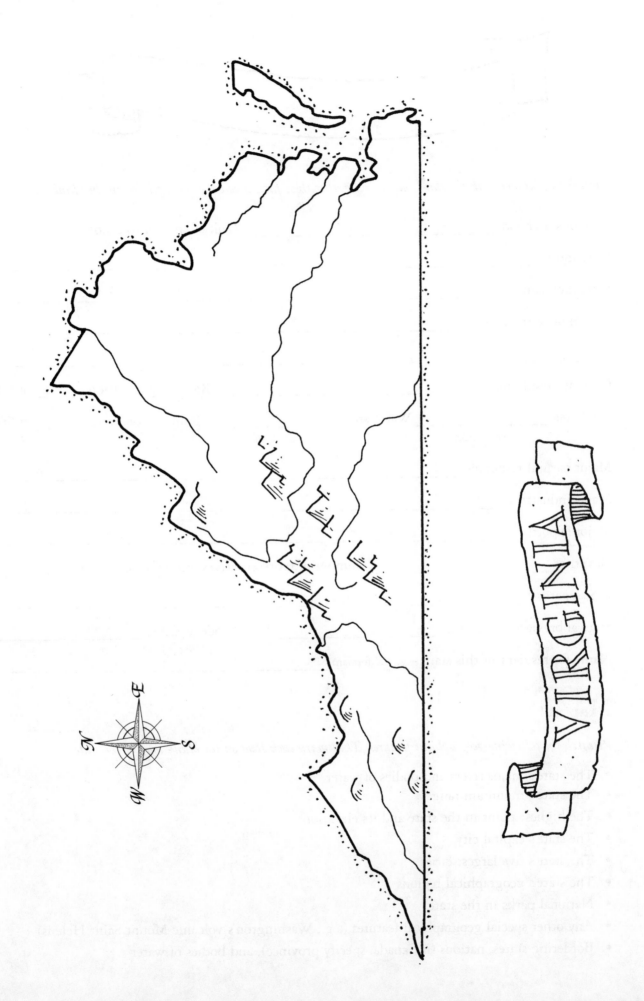

VIRGINIA

Decorate the banner with the state's name and gather these facts about the state, filling in the blanks.

Date of statehood _____ Rank of entry into union _____ of 50

State motto _____

State nickname _____

Origin of state name _____

_____

Current population _____ Rank in population _____ of 50

Land area _____ Water area _____ Rank in total area _____ of 50
       (square miles)   *(square miles)*

Major natural resources _____

Major industries _____

Major exports _____

Governor _____ Number of representatives elected to U.S. Congress _____

U.S. senators _____

State abbreviation (e.g., Ariz.) _____ Postal code (e.g., AZ) _____

Name for resident of this state (e.g., Californian) _____

Map It!

Research the following geographical features. Then mark each item on the blank map of the state.

- The state's major rivers and bodies of water
- The state's mountain ranges
- The highest point in the state and its elevation
- The state's capital city
- The state's five largest cities
- The state's geographical regions
- National parks in the state
- Any other special geographical features (e.g., Washington's volcanic Mount Saint Helens)
- Bordering states, nations (if Canada, specify province), and bodies of water

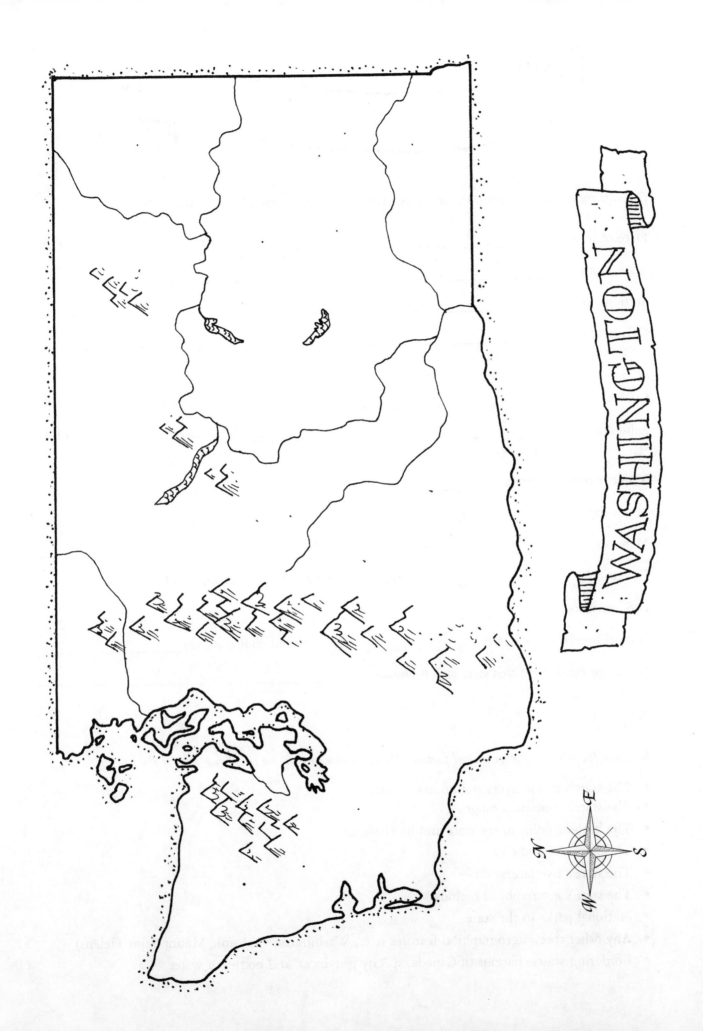

Decorate the banner with the state's name and gather these facts about the state, filling in the blanks.

Date of statehood _____ Rank of entry into union _____ of 50

State motto _____

State nickname _____

Origin of state name _____

_____

Current population _____ Rank in population _____ of 50

Land area _____ Water area _____ Rank in total area _____ of 50
     (square miles)   *(square miles)*

Major natural resources _____

Major industries _____

Major exports _____

Governor _____ Number of representatives elected to U.S. Congress _____

U.S. senators _____

State abbreviation (e.g., Ariz.) _____ Postal code (e.g., AZ) _____

Name for resident of this state (e.g., Californian) _____

Map It!

Research the following geographical features. Then mark each item on the blank map of the state.

- The state's major rivers and bodies of water
- The state's mountain ranges
- The highest point in the state and its elevation
- The state's capital city
- The state's five largest cities
- The state's geographical regions
- National parks in the state
- Any other special geographical features (e.g., Washington's volcanic Mount Saint Helens)
- Bordering states, nations (if Canada, specify province), and bodies of water

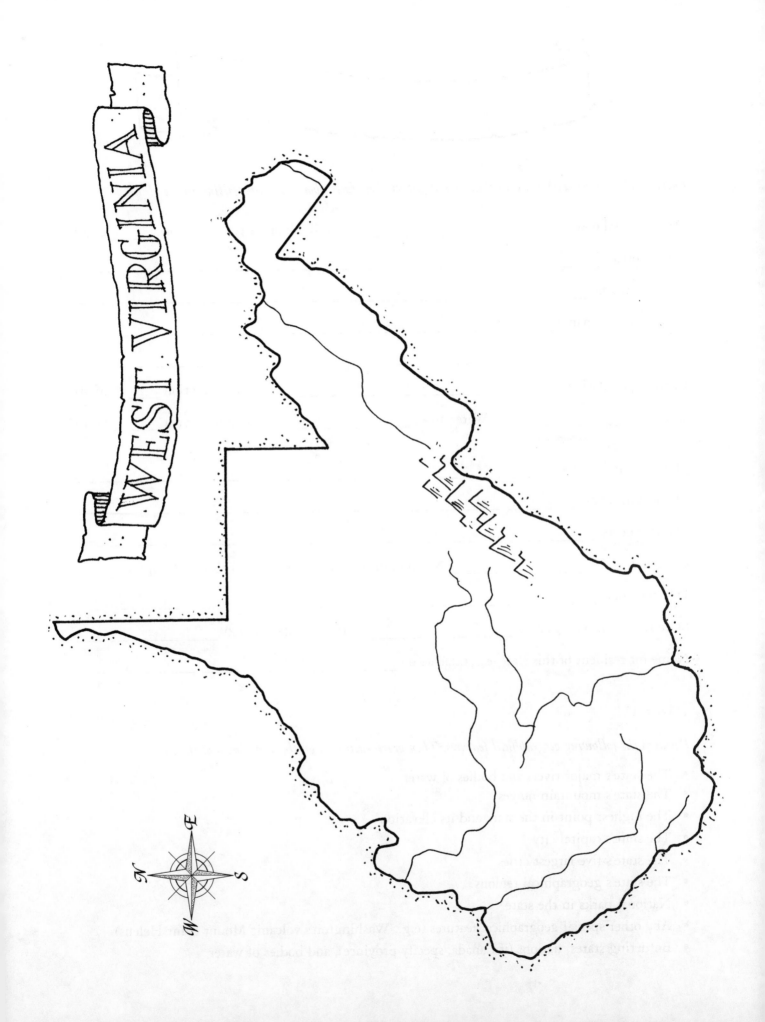

WEST VIRGINIA

Decorate the banner with the state's name and gather these facts about the state, filling in the blanks.

Date of statehood _____ Rank of entry into union _____ of 50

State motto _____

State nickname _____

Origin of state name _____

_____

Current population _____ Rank in population _____ of 50

Land area _____ Water area _____ Rank in total area _____ of 50
      (square miles)   *(square miles)*

Major natural resources _____

Major industries _____

Major exports _____

Governor _____ Number of representatives elected to U.S. Congress _____

U.S. senators _____

State abbreviation (e.g., Ariz.) _____ Postal code (e.g., AZ) _____

Name for resident of this state (e.g., Californian) _____

Map It!

Research the following geographical features. Then mark each item on the blank map of the state.

- The state's major rivers and bodies of water
- The state's mountain ranges
- The highest point in the state and its elevation
- The state's capital city
- The state's five largest cities
- The state's geographical regions
- National parks in the state
- Any other special geographical features (e.g., Washington's volcanic Mount Saint Helens)
- Bordering states, nations (if Canada, specify province), and bodies of water

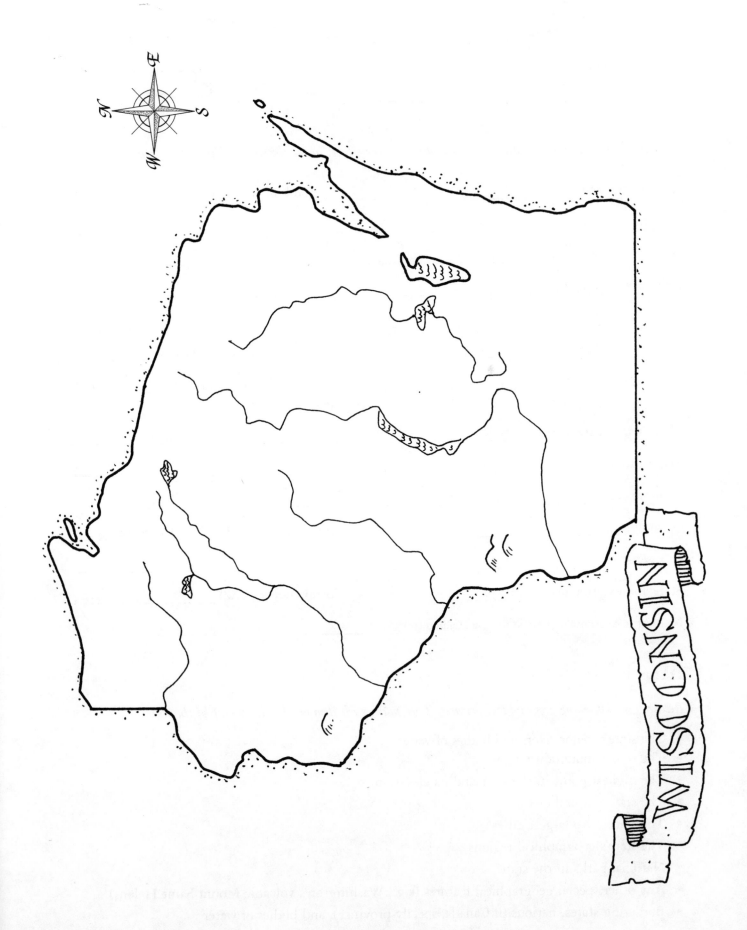

Decorate the banner with the state's name and gather these facts about the state, filling in the blanks.

Date of statehood _____ Rank of entry into union _____ of 50

State motto _____

State nickname _____

Origin of state name _____

_____

Current population _____ Rank in population _____ of 50

Land area _____ Water area _____ Rank in total area _____ of 50
   (square miles)   *(square miles)*

Major natural resources _____

Major industries _____

Major exports _____

Governor _____ Number of representatives elected to U.S. Congress _____

U.S. senators _____

State abbreviation (e.g., Ariz.) _____ Postal code (e.g., AZ) _____

Name for resident of this state (e.g., Californian) _____

Map It!

Research the following geographical features. Then mark each item on the blank map of the state.

- The state's major rivers and bodies of water
- The state's mountain ranges
- The highest point in the state and its elevation
- The state's capital city
- The state's five largest cities
- The state's geographical regions
- National parks in the state
- Any other special geographical features (e.g., Washington's volcanic Mount Saint Helens)
- Bordering states, nations (if Canada, specify province), and bodies of water

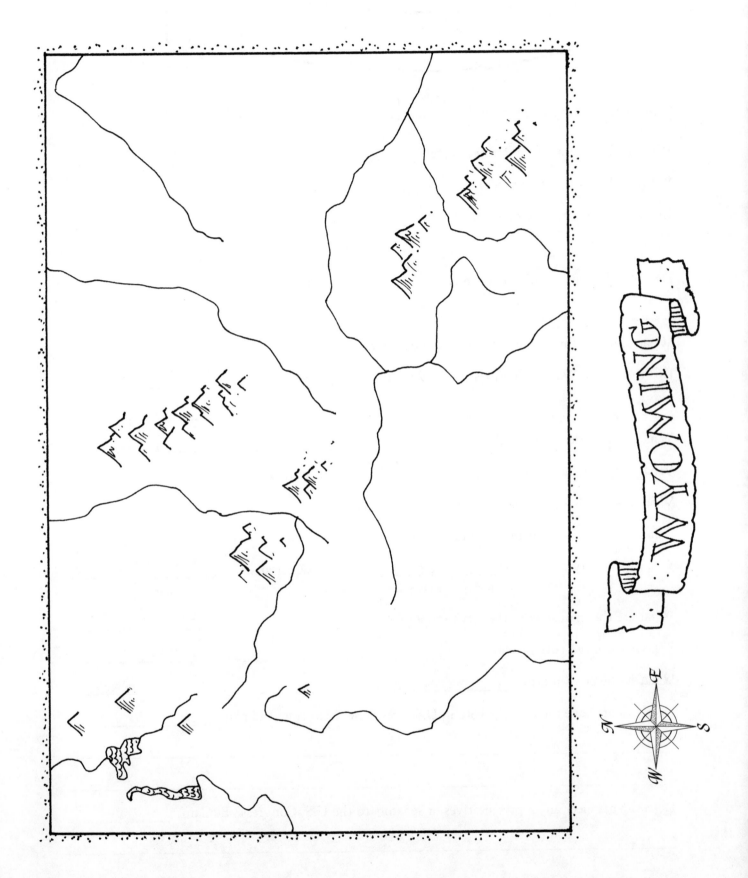

Decorate the banner with the capital's name and gather these facts about it, filling in the blanks.

What is the capital of the United States? _____

What is the origin of its name? _____

Describe the location of the capital. _____

_____

Describe the relationship between the city of Washington and the District of Columbia. _____

_____

What year was this site selected by Congress as the future capital? _____

Did the city of Washington exist then? Explain. _____

_____

What states ceded land for the new capital? _____

What year was the seat of government moved from Philadelphia? _____

Who was the first president to live in the White House? _____

What is the capital's current population and ranking among U.S. cities? _____

What is the city's land area? _____ Water area? _____
                  (square miles)   *(square miles)*

What are the mainstays of the city's economy? _____

Who is the city's current mayor? _____

What is the city's motto? _____

Do residents have the right to vote in U.S. presidential elections? Explain. _____

_____

_____

Do residents elect any representatives or senators to the U.S. Congress? Explain _____

_____

_____

APPENDIX A

Historical Mapping Activities

The additional maps and mapping instructions in this appendix allow the student to learn more about the history of the United States through mapping activities related to (1) the Thirteen Colonies and the American Revolution, (2) the Louisiana Purchase, and (3) the Civil War. The pages are designed so that they can be used directly by the student. However, you may choose to modify the mapping directions according to the student's age and depth of study of these historical periods. Available free of charge through many libraries, the online subscription sites *America the Beautiful*, *Lands and Peoples*, and *American Indian History and Culture* have good historical maps. The free site www.bartleby.com has the text of many relevant American historical documents, including those related to the Louisiana Purchase. Many Heroes of History biographies and Unit Study Curriculum Guides cover these time periods, including those for William Penn, Benjamin Franklin, George Washington, John Adams, Meriwether Lewis, Abraham Lincoln, Harriet Tubman, and Clara Barton. For more about these and other resources, see Appendix E.

Map It!

Mark the following items on the blank map of the Thirteen Colonies, also called the Thirteen Original States.

- The Thirteen Colonies: New Hampshire, Massachusetts (both parts), Rhode Island, Connecticut, New York, New Jersey, Pennsylvania, Delaware, Maryland, Virginia, North Carolina, South Carolina, Georgia

- The Atlantic Ocean

- The Proclamation Line of 1763

- Indian Country

- The locations of selected Native American lands: Penobscot, Mahican, Iroquois, Wampanoag, Massachuset, Pawtucket, Lenni Lenape, Shawnee, Powhatan, Pequot, Cherokee, Creek, Yamasee

- The Ohio Valley

- Selected forts: Fort Duquesne, Fort Necessity, Fort William Henry, Fort Niagara

- Selected settlements and cities important to colonial America and the American Revolution

  New Hampshire: Dover, Portsmouth, Manchester, Concord
  Massachusetts: Plymouth, Salem, Boston
  Rhode Island: Providence, Newport, Warwick
  Connecticut: Wethersfield, Hartford, New Haven
  New York: New York, Ticonderoga
  New Jersey: Trenton, Princeton, Monmouth
  Pennsylvania: Philadelphia, Valley Forge
  Delaware: Lewes, Wilmington, Dover
  Maryland: Annapolis, Baltimore
  Virginia: Jamestown, Williamsburg, Richmond, Yorktown
  North Carolina: Charlotte, New Bern, Salem
  South Carolina: Charleston, Georgetown, Beaufort
  Georgia: Savannah

- U.S. Capitals: Philadelphia, Pennsylvania; New York, New York; Washington, D.C.

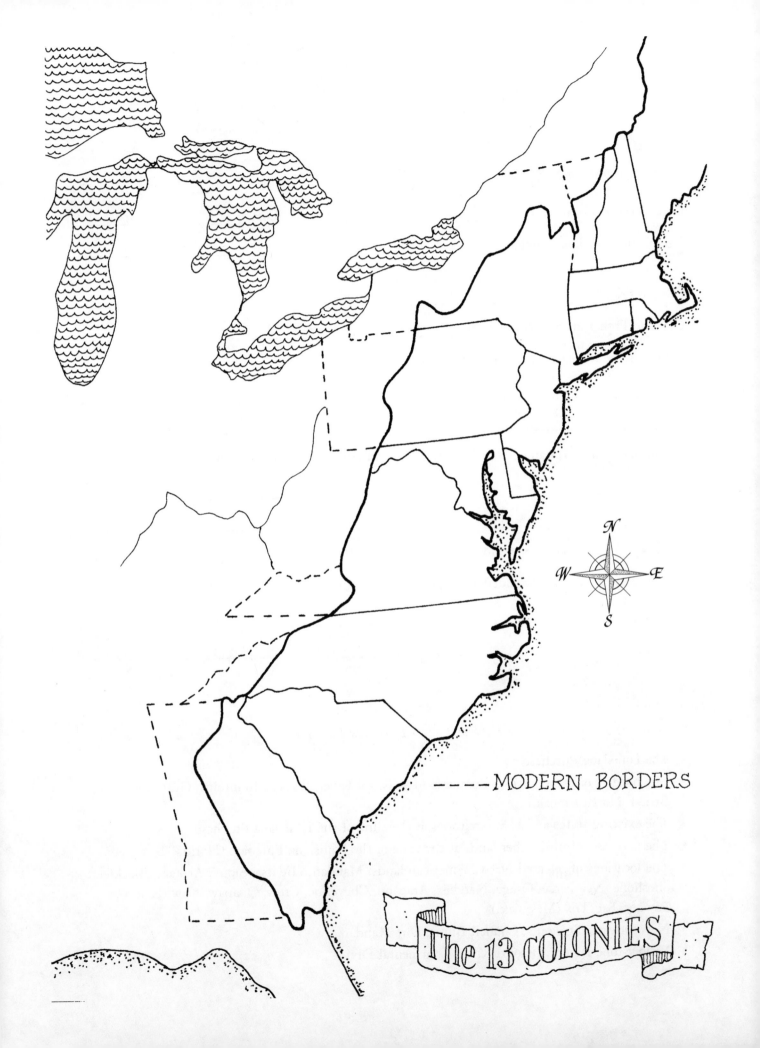

----- MODERN BORDERS

The 13 COLONIES

Gather these facts about the Louisiana Purchase, filling in the blanks.

Date of the Louisiana Purchase _____ Cost _____

Size of the Louisiana Purchase _____ _____

                                     in square miles   *in relation to existing U.S.*

U.S. president _____ French leader _____

U.S. and French ministers involved _____

Why was the Louisiana Purchase important to the United States? _____

_____

_____

Whom had France obtained Louisiana from, and why was France willing to sell it? _____

_____

_____

Who were the official U.S. explorers of the Louisiana Purchase? _____

The Louisiana Purchase included all or part of what fourteen present-day states? _____

_____

_____

Map It!

Mark the following items on the blank map of the Louisiana Purchase.

- The Louisiana Purchase
- The borders of the Louisiana Purchase: Mississippi River, Rocky Mountains, Gulf of Mexico, British North America
- The existing states and U.S. territories at the time of the Louisiana Purchase
- The nations claiming other lands at the time of the Louisiana Purchase (Florida, Texas, etc.)
- The locations of selected Native American lands: Mandan, Hidatsa, Sioux, Arikara, Blackfeet, Shoshone, Nez Perce, Osage, Natchez, Arapaho, Cheyenne, Crow, Quapaw, Kaw (Kansa), Pawnee, Sac, Fox (Mesquaki)
- New Orleans, St. Louis, Council Bluffs, Fort Mandan
- Yellowstone River, Missouri River, Continental Divide

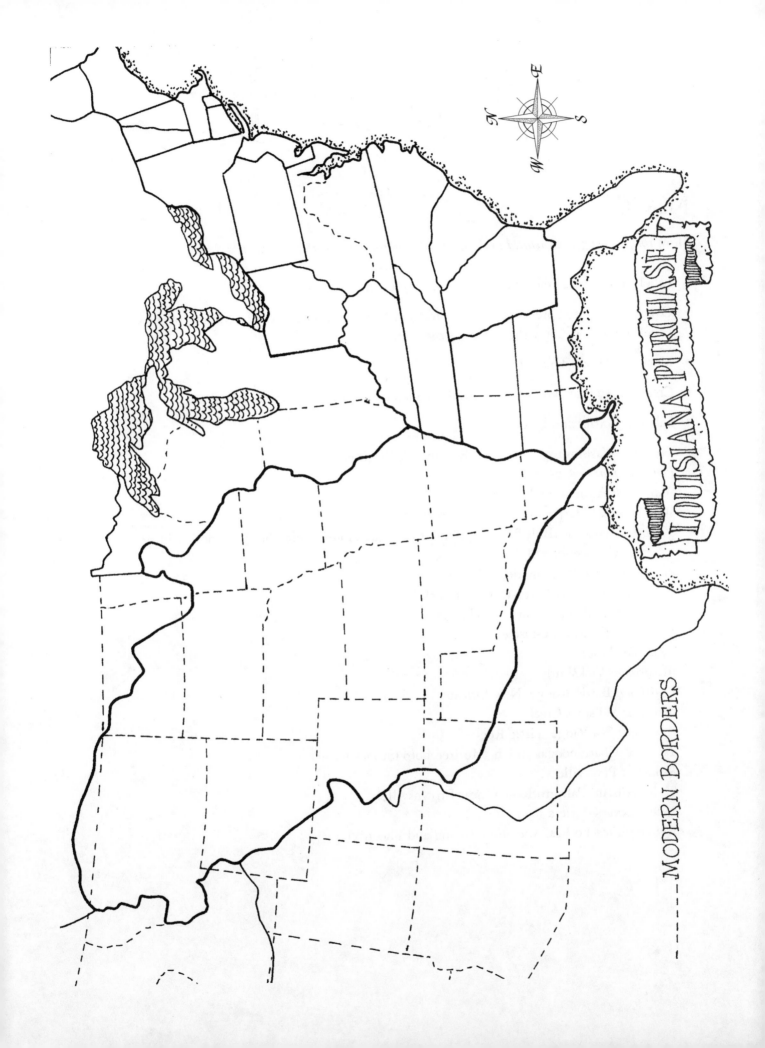

LOUISIANA PURCHASE

----- MODERN BORDERS

Map It!

Mark the following items related to the Civil War on the blank map of the United States.

- Label the existing states as of the beginning of the Civil War.

- Overlay the state borders with the borders of U.S. territories at the beginning of the Civil War. Label the map to show the names of the territories.

- Mark the Mason-Dixon Line.

- Create a key that shows Union and Confederate states and slave and free states.

- Label key cities and battle sites:

  Capitals: Washington, D.C., and Richmond, Virginia
  Pennsylvania: Gettysburg
  Maryland: Antietam (Sharpsburg)
  West Virginia: Harpers Ferry
  Virginia: Manassas (Bull Run), Appomattox Court House, Petersburg, Fredericksburg, Chancellorsville
  North Carolina: Bentonville, Wilmington
  South Carolina: Charleston (Fort Sumter), Columbia
  Georgia: Savannah, Atlanta, Chickamauga
  Florida: Tallahassee, Olustee
  Alabama: Mobile
  Mississippi: Vicksburg
  Louisiana: Baton Rouge, New Orleans
  Missouri: Wilson's Creek
  Arkansas: Pea Ridge, Little Rock
  Tennessee: Chattanooga, Shiloh, Murfreesboro (Stones River)
  Kentucky: Perryville
  Texas: Austin, Palmito Ranch (near Brownsville)
  New Mexico: Glorieta Pass
  Arizona: Picacho Peak (between Tucson and Phoenix)

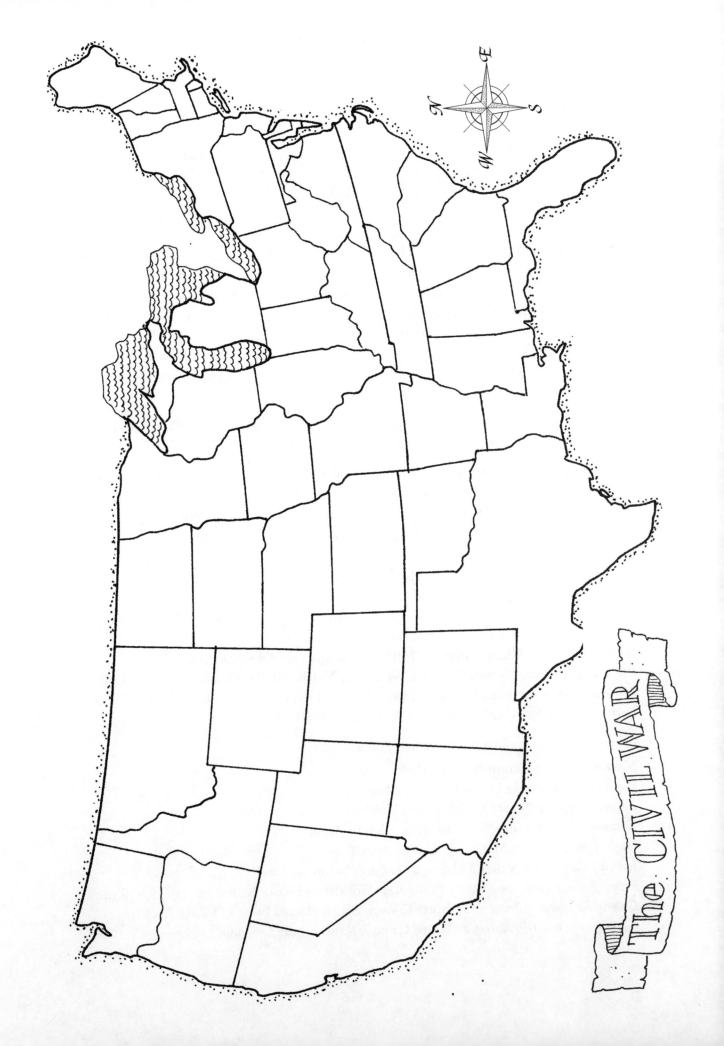

The CIVIL WAR

APPENDIX B

Additional Mapping Activities for the United States

Students can use the blank map of the U.S. to mark many different places, trends, and events, from labeling the fifty states and their capitals to plotting the nation's geographical features to tracing key periods in history. Even if a student is using *Maps of the United States* as a workbook, we suggest that you photocopy the extra map of the United States (see page 128) before it is used so that he or she can undertake more than one activity.

Note that two mapping activities can be done on the same map to show the relationship between them, for example, the relationship between the nation's geography and the distribution of natural resources, industries, and agricultural products.

- Label the fifty states and their capitals. Include the nation's capital, Washington, D.C. (The teacher may want students to also include each state's largest city.)

- Using colored pencils, outline and lightly shade each region of the United States in a different color. Label the regions, the states, and each region's three largest cities. (The teacher can select which regional groupings to use. The following is one of several common groupings.)

  New England States: Connecticut, Maine, Massachusetts, New Hampshire, Rhode Island, Vermont

  Mid-Atlantic States: Delaware, Maryland, New Jersey, New York, Pennsylvania

  South-Central States: Arkansas, Kentucky, Tennessee, West Virginia

  Southern States: Alabama, Florida, Georgia, Louisiana, Mississippi, North Carolina, South Carolina, Texas, Virginia

  Great Lakes States: Illinois, Indiana, Michigan, Minnesota, Ohio, Wisconsin

  Plains States: Iowa, Kansas, Missouri, Nebraska, North Dakota, Oklahoma, South Dakota

  Mountain States: Arizona, Colorado, Idaho, Montana, Nevada, New Mexico, Utah, Wyoming

  Pacific States: Alaska, California, Hawaii, Oregon, Washington

- Label the extreme points of the United States:

  Northernmost point: Point Barrow, Alaska

  Southernmost point: Ka Lae (South Cape), Hawaii

  Easternmost point: West Quoddy Head, Maine

  Westernmost point: Cape Wrangell (Attu Island), Alaska

  Highest point: Mount McKinley, Alaska, 20,320 feet

  Lowest point: Death Valley, California, 282 feet below sea level

  Points farthest apart: Log Point, Elliot Key, Florida, and Kure Island, Hawaii, 5,859 mi.

  Geographic center (50 states): in Butte County, South Dakota (west of Castle Rock)

  Geographic center (48 states): in Smith County, Kansas (near Lebanon)

- Indicate and label the nation's major mountain ranges, rivers, coastal waters, and other bodies of water. Mark the Continental Divide.

- Gather information about the key natural resources, industries, and agricultural products of the different regions of the United States. Construct a key that represents them (e.g., a tree for timber or sunglasses for tourism). Label the map of the United States accordingly.

- Construct a key for population density. Color the map of the United States accordingly.

- Construct a key for average annual precipitation. Color the map of the United States accordingly.

- Map the expansion of the United States. Using a colored pencil, draw the boundary line of the Thirteen Original States. Then draw the borders of later land pieces acquired by the United States. Make a key showing who the U.S. acquired the land from and the date. Shade the map accordingly. (*Lands and Peoples* is a good source. See Appendix E.)

- Map the geological features and routes important to the expansion of the United States. Include the Appalachian Mountains, Mississippi River, Rocky Mountains, Cumberland Gap, Wilderness Road, Natchez Trace, Sante Fe Trail, Oregon Trail, and first transcontinental railroad. Label the cities or sites important to these routes, such as Independence, Missouri, and Sante Fe, New Mexico.

- Label each of the fifty states with its name and the date of its entry into the union.

- Label the states that existed at the beginning of the Lewis and Clark expedition. Using colored pencils, overlay the other modern state borders with the borders of U.S. territories and areas claimed by other nations. Map the westward and eastbound journeys of Lewis and Clark, including rivers, mountains, and other geographical features they encountered. Indicate the Native American tribes they met (Mandan, Hidatsa, Sioux, Arikara, Blackfeet, Shoshone, Nez Perce, Chinook) as well as their methods of transportation and the places where they wintered. Include animals they encountered, such as buffalo, grizzlies, and salmon.

- The idea of an "Indian Country" separating Native Americans from white settlers began in colonial times and extended through the expansion of the United States. The boundaries of Indian Country were redefined several times. Using colored pencils, map the changing Indian Country, also called Indian Territory. Include the Proclamation Line of 1763, Appalachian Mountains, Mississippi River, Missouri River, and Red River. Show the Cherokee Trail of Tears. You could also show other "trails of tears," such as those of the Choctaw, Chickasaw, Creek, and Seminole. (*American Indian History and Culture* is a good source. See Appendix E.)

APPENDIX C

Student Explorations

These diverse activities provide students of different ages and different learning styles with the forum to delve deeper into learning about the fifty states as well as the nation's capital and U.S. dependencies. The activities require varying amounts of research and can be made more or less comprehensive at your discretion. Where necessary, you can alter the directions, give additional instructions, or provide specific ideas for the particular state being studied. Choose the activities that are best suited to your student or students.

- Make a topographical model of the state using dough, clay, or papier mâché. Form and label the state's major rivers and bodies of water, mountain ranges, plains, deserts, and other geographical characteristics. In addition, label the state capital, the state's five largest cities, and three other important sites of your choice. Note that *The Stuff That Fun Is Made Of* by Selena LaPorte, also published by Emerald Books, has an excellent collection of easy recipes and instructions for making homemade doughs and paints for landscape and relief maps, including those for making the base, water, mountains, deserts and plains, and even volcanoes. See Appendix E.

- Find a picture of the state's flag in a book or online. Research the symbolism behind the flag's design. Then draw or paint a picture of the flag and write a paragraph explaining what the different elements of the design represent.

- Create a collage about the state. From old newspapers and magazines, cut out words, letters, and pictures that relate to the state's history, geography, economy, and current events. Plan your design and then glue the cutouts to a large piece of paper so that it is completely covered. Be sure to include the state's name and year of statehood.

- Make a brochure or poster encouraging people to move to the state. Include interesting facts and descriptions of the state's people, history, geography, climate, and economy that might entice others to move there. Be sure to include both pictures and words and use lots of color.

- Make a historical timeline for the state on a long sheet of paper or by joining several smaller sheets together. Include Native American nations, European and U.S. exploration and settlement, the lives of famous state residents, and major events in the state's history. Include the date of statehood and, if applicable, the date the U.S. acquired the land and the date the territory was organized. To put things in perspective, add three or four major national and world events as well as the lives of a few key historical figures from outside the state.

- Pick a key historical event in the state that you think makes a good story and write a skit or play about it. Act it out or create a video production.

- Write a newspaper article about a key historical event in the state. For a larger project or for a group project, create a whole newspaper about key events in the state, both historical and current. Begin by studying a real newspaper to see how articles are composed.

- Write a report that traces the state's history to the current day. Report on people and events leading to statehood, such as Native American nations, European and U.S. exploration and settlement, any disputes over the territory, and how the U.S. acquired the territory. Then report on several key events since statehood. Finally, provide a current look at life in the state today.

- Write a report about the state, focusing on life in the state today. Include information about the state's people and culture, geography, climate, animal and plant life, and economy. Be sure to include good descriptions and interesting facts so that your readers will learn what makes this state unique.

- Imagine you are living in the state's largest city at the time the state entered the union. First decide who you are (e.g., child or adult, man or woman, occupation). Then write a series of journal entries that show what daily life is like for you. Reflect on an issue important to your state's residents and on your state's entry into the union. Include descriptions of your surroundings, in nature and in the city, so that future generations can envision your life.

- Write a travel essay about the state or one of its important cities. First read examples of travel writing. (These kinds of creative essays can be found in magazines, books of essays, and the travel sections of newspapers.) Then research the state or city and re-create a trip in writing, with descriptions of what you saw, who you met, what you ate, and how you traveled. Think about all your senses. What did you see, hear, smell, feel, and taste? You may want to focus on one interesting city, or you might want to lead your readers on a tour of the state's different regions or famous places. If you really have visited the state, that's great, but your trip can be imaginary.

- Interview someone who has lived in this state and, using stories, facts, and quotations from your interview, write a creative essay that shares the person's experiences and thoughts about life in this state. First work with an adult to arrange the interview. The interview could be in person, on the phone, over email, or through the mail. Then read examples of published character sketches. (These kinds of creative essays can be found in magazines, newspaper features, and books of essays.) Next, prepare your list of questions, being sure to include a variety of topics. Depending on what you've arranged, send your questions to the person or refer to the list during your conversation. If the interview is in person, request permission to record it to help you in your writing.

- Write and illustrate a picture book that introduces younger children to the state. What essential facts should they know? What about the state will catch their interest? What makes the state unique? What would they like to see illustrated? Be sure to include a front and back cover. When your book is done, read it to a younger child.

- Write and illustrate a picture book about a famous person from the state whom you find very interesting. What interests you about this person? Is there something unique about him or her? What is this person famous for? What has he or she contributed and achieved? Has being from this state made a difference in this person's life or a difference for the state? Ask yourself questions like these and then tell the person's story in your own words and with your own illustrations. Be sure to make a front and back cover for your book. When your book is done, read it aloud to others.

- Prepare and give an oral presentation about a Native American tribe whose home was on this land at the time of colonial or U.S. settlement. Research the tribe's culture and daily life at that time. Investigate the tribe's relationships with settlers and the U.S. and/or colonial government. Trace the tribe's history since the time of settlement and find out about the people's lives today. Create a visual aid to use in your presentation.

- Prepare and give an oral report about a particular ethnic or immigrant group that settled in the state in large numbers. Why did they settle there? What hardships did they face? What contributions did they make? What are their lives like today?

- Research the history of Washington, D.C., and its role as the capital of the United States. Write a report or give an oral presentation about what you discover.

- Research how Washington, D.C., has been governed in the past, how it is governed today, and how its residents are represented in the national government. Learn about the district's efforts to become a state. Imagine that you will be making a presentation before Congress in an effort to win its support of statehood for the District of Columbia. Be sure to address the objections of those who want the nation's capital to remain a district. Optional: Create a computer slide show to use during your oral presentation.

- Prepare and give an oral presentation on one of the current territories or commonwealths of the United States. Find out about its people, geography, and economy. How is the territory or commonwealth governed? What rights and responsibilities does it share with the states? What is different? Learn about its history before and after becoming associated with the U.S. and how the association began. Investigate how the relationship benefits each party and whether the relationship has been a detriment for either party in any way. Create visual aids, including a map that shows the location of the territory or commonwealth, to use in your presentation.

- Puerto Rico is a commonwealth associated with the United States. Puerto Ricans were given U.S. citizenship in 1917, yet Puerto Rico is not a state. Puerto Ricans have voted several times about becoming an independent nation, becoming a state, or remaining a commonwealth, choosing each time to keep their current relationship with the United States. Research the different sides of the debate. What are the arguments for independence? What are the arguments for statehood? What are the arguments for retaining commonwealth status? Prepare and give a persuasive speech or write a persuasive essay in support of one of the three positions. Whether you give a speech or write an essay, be sure to address the arguments of the opposing views. Alternative option: Work with one or two other students and stage a debate, with each student advocating one point of view.

APPENDIX D

Conceptual Social Studies Exercises

To complete these brief conceptual activities, students can write one or more paragraphs in response, present an oral report on one of the topics, or discuss the answers to one or more activities in a group context. Note that some activities may not be suited to all fifty states.

- Name and locate two states that are larger than this state in area, two that are about the same size, and two that are smaller. Do the same for population.

- Compare the population of the state's largest city with other cities around the United States. Name two cities that are about the same size.

- Calculate the state's population density in people per square mile. How does it compare with surrounding states' population densities?

- Compare the population of the state to the total population of the United States. Express this comparison as a percentage.

- Study a physical map of the state. Where do you think most of the population would live? Why? Use a population map to test your hypothesis. Were you right or wrong? Explain.

- Research a natural disaster that the state is prone to. How is this hazard related to the state's geography? How do people protect themselves against it?

- Study a map that shows the annual average precipitation in the state. Is the amount of precipitation consistent across the state? If so, why might this be? If not, how does it vary and why do you think this is? How does the amount of precipitation relate to the state's geography?

- Study maps that show the population density and annual average precipitation across the United States. Is there any relationship between precipitation and population? Why do you think this is?

APPENDIX E

Resources

Many excellent resources are available for studying the fifty states. In addition to the wealth of sources available in libraries for individual states, the resources listed here include books, Internet sites, and subscription sites available through many libraries and schools. As with all material for your students, you will want to preview the sources yourself.

Books

These are just some of the many good books available. There may be some here that you'd like to add to your own list of favorites.

The Stuff That Fun Is Made Of: A Comprehensive Collection of Recipes for Play and Learning

Author: Selena LaPorte
Publication: Lynnwood, Wash.: Emerald Books, 2001
ISBN: 188300277X
Description: 160 pages

Summary: *The Stuff That Fun Is Made Of* is a collection of more than ninety recipes and suggestions for more than one hundred arts and crafts projects and learning activities. It contains simple, inexpensive recipes and instructions for making homemade landscape and relief map doughs and paints. In addition, you'll find specific instructions for making blue-water dough, dough that's good for forming mountains, and a dough especially for deserts and plains. Students can form the shape of the state, fill in rivers and lakes, and build up mountain ranges, even volcanoes.

National Geographic United States Atlas for Young Explorers

Author: National Geographic Society (U.S.)
Publication: Washington, D.C.: National Geographic Society, 2004
ISBN: 0792268407
Description: 176 pages, ages 8–12

Summary: National Geographic produces excellent material that is highly recommended by children's librarians. A good source for student research, this atlas contains U.S. and state maps, photo essays, and illustrations that present information about the regions and states of the United States as well as U.S. territories.

National Geographic Our Fifty States

Authors: Mark H. Bockenhauer and Stephen F. Cunha
Publication: Washington, D.C.: National Geographic Society, 2004
ISBN: 0792264029
Description: 240 pages, young adult

Summary: Filled with more than three hundred illustrations and photographs, fun facts, concise essays by two professors of geography, and specially designed maps, this authoritative guide reveals fascinating details behind each state's unique history, climate, resources, and more. It is organized by region and includes Washington, D.C., and U.S. territories.

Macmillan Color Atlas of the States

Author: Mark T. Mattson
Publication: New York: Macmillan Library Reference USA, 1996
ISBN: 0028646592
Description: 377 pages, high school and up

Summary: A cross between an atlas and an encyclopedia, this well-designed and well-researched resource devotes seven pages to each state. It includes more than three hundred color maps and charts and is arranged alphabetically. The maps, text, and easy-to-read tables present information about each state's history, geography, economy, demography, culture, and government. Washington, D.C., is also covered.

The National Atlas of the United States of America

Author: Geological Survey (U.S.)
Publication: Reston, Va.: U.S. Dept. of the Interior; U.S. Geological Survey, Denver, Colo., 2002
ISBN: 0607986697

Summary: This reference work shows all fifty states at the same scale, making actual size comparisons visually possible. The atlas includes an alphabetical listing of states with their areas, populations, and highest and lowest points; a listing of U.S. rivers, lakes, mountains, and islands; and color photographs of various places of interest. An online version is on the Internet at www.nationalatlas.gov (see Internet Sites).

The New Big Book of America

Authors: Todd Davis and Marc Frey
Publication: Philadelphia: Courage Books, 2002
ISBN: 0762412631
Description: 56 pages, ages 8–12

Summary: This young reader's guide to the history, geography, and culture of all fifty states is another high quality source. With one large page for every state, each entry includes a small but informative topographical map of the state, a few photos or illustrations, basic facts, a brief essay, and two sidebars highlighting people, events, movements, or places that have been influential in the state's history.

Don't Know Much About the Fifty States

Author: Kenneth C. Davis
Illustrator: Renee Andriani
Publication: New York: HarperCollins Publishers, 2001
ISBN: 0060286075
Description: 61 pages, ages 8–12

Summary: Each page of this colorful book is devoted to one state and includes a core set of information (nickname, date of statehood, capital, state flower, state bird, and postal abbreviation), with the majority of the page presenting unique facts about the state in a question-and-answer format. While the book doesn't include enough information for use as a student's only source, the information it does contain definitely piques the interest.

The Train of States

Author: Peter Sís
Publication: New York: Greenwillow Books, 2004

ISBN: 0060578386
Description: 64 pages, ages 7–10

Summary: In this train of circus wagons conducted by Uncle Sam, each state is represented by one car, appearing in order of statehood, with Washington, D.C., as the caboose. In this imaginative picture-book format, Peter Sís presents information about each state, including its capital, motto, state tree, state bird, source of name, and date of statehood. This book won the American Library Association Notable Books for Children award for 2005.

The Scrambled States of America

Author/Illustrator: Laurie Keller
Publication: New York: Henry Holt, 1998
ISBN: 0805058028
Description: 40 pages, ages 8–10

Summary: Disenchanted with their fixed places on the map, the states decide to swap spots in hopes that each can get to see a different part of the country and do something different for a change. This picture book is full of facts and fun. Children will have a geography lesson like never before. A movie is also available. (See Movie.)

Heroes of History Biography Series

Authors: Janet and Geoff Benge
Publication: Lynnwood, Wash.: Emerald Books, 2001–2005
Description: 192–224 pages each, ages 10 and up

Summary: Written in an engaging narrative style, the Heroes of History biographies tell the fascinating life stories of men and women who changed the course of American history. Their fast-paced adventure style and consistent historical depth have made them favorites of kids and grownups alike. These biographies inspired the creation of *Maps of the United States* at the prompting of teachers who use them. Geared for independent readers ages ten and up, these books also make good read-alouds for younger children. The authors, Janet and Geoff Benge, are a husband and wife writing team with twenty years of writing experience. Janet is a former elementary school teacher. Geoff holds a degree in history. Together they have a passion to make history come alive for a new generation of readers. As of printing, the following biographies are available, with more coming:

Christopher Columbus: Across the Ocean Sea • 1-932096-23-X
William Penn: Liberty and Justice for All • 1-883002-82-6
Benjamin Franklin: Live Wire • 1-932096-14-0
George Washington: True Patriot • 1-883002-81-8
John Adams: Independence Forever • 1-883002-51-6
Daniel Boone: Frontiersman • 1-932096-09-4
Meriwether Lewis: Off the Edge of the Map • 1-883002-80-X
Abraham Lincoln: A New Birth of Freedom • 1-883002-79-6
Harriet Tubman: Freedombound • 1-883002-90-7
Clara Barton: Courage under Fire • 1-883002-50-8
George Washington Carver: From Slave to Scientist • 1-883002-78-8
Laura Ingalls Wilder: A Storybook Life • 1-932096-32-9 (Fall 2005)
Theodore Roosevelt: An American Original • 1-932096-10-8
Douglas MacArthur: What Greater Honor • 1-932096-15-9

Heroes of History Unit Study Curriculum Guides

Authors: Janet and Geoff Benge
Publication: Lynnwood, Wash.: Emerald Books, 2001–2005
Description: 64 pages each

Summary: Each Heroes of History Unit Study Curriculum Guide is designed to accompany a Heroes of History biography. These guides provide the schoolteacher and homeschooling parent with a variety of ways to teach diverse curriculum areas as they relate to the life of a key historical figure. Each guide is designed for a variety of learning styles, grade levels, and abilities and for both individual and group study. Teachers choose from an array of options to build a meaningful unit study. As of printing, the following guides are available, with more coming:

William Penn: A Unit Study Curriculum Guide • 1-883002-87-7
George Washington: A Unit Study Curriculum Guide • 1-883002-86-9
Daniel Boone: A Unit Study Curriculum Guide • 1932096-29-9 *(Fall 2005)*
Meriwether Lewis: A Unit Study Curriculum Guide • 1-883002-85-0
Abraham Lincoln: A Unit Study Curriculum Guide • 1-883002-84-2
Harriet Tubman: A Unit Study Curriculum Guide • 1-883002-99-0
George Washington Carver: A Unit Study Curriculum Guide • 1-883002-83-4
Theodore Roosevelt: A Unit Study Curriculum Guide • 1-932096-30-2 *(Fall 2005)*

The Uniting States: The Story of Statehood for the Fifty United States

Editor: Benjamin F. Shearer
Publication: Westport, Conn.: Greenwood Press, 2004
ISBN: 0313327033
Description: 1,434 pages (3 volumes), adult

Summary: This reference work is suitable for advanced high-school students or for the teacher's own research. Fifty-one essays and over ninety maps tell the story of how each of the fifty states in the Union became and remained part of one nation over a span of 172 years. The contributors teach American history at the college level.

Internet Sites

In addition to the official websites of the fifty states (see www.usa.gov), these are some of the excellent online sources for learning about the the United States and U.S. dependencies.

www.usa.gov

This U.S. government website includes links to the official website of each of the fifty states. Along with information for residents, the state websites include state facts and history. Many have special sections for students.

www.nationalatlas.gov

Be sure to check out this site. This is not like any atlas you remember! Together with more than twenty other federal organizations, the U.S. Geological Survey (USGS) has created a new, online edition of *The National Atlas of the United States of America*. On this interactive site you can customize your own map for printing or viewing, print pre-formatted maps on a variety of topics, order wall maps, play with interactive maps, and learn about historical events like the Civil War.

An exciting feature of this site is its ability to create a map of the U.S. according to one or more selected themes. You can then view the whole U.S., zoom in, or select certain states. Themes include state boundaries, state names, capitals, cities and towns, counties, average annual precipitation, population and population density, natural disasters, agriculture, biology, history, time zones, Indian lands, geological features, environmental issues, latitude and longitude, economy, and health.

www.cia.gov/cia/publications/factbook

This is the online version of *The World Factbook,* the U.S. government's geographical handbook featuring profiles, full-color maps, and flags of all the nations. Individual states are not covered, but the *The World Factbook* has good entries on the United States and U.S. dependencies.

www.yale.edu/lawweb/avalon/avalon.htm

The website of Yale University's Avalon Project is a treasure trove of U.S. and other historical documents sorted by century. Though it's easy enough to use, the site is not meant for young children. Teachers and advanced older students—particularly curious ones—will find items of interest relevant to the study of the United States. Among a multitude of others, the documents available include the Royal Proclamation of 1763, the Treaty of Paris, the papers of George Washington, the Emancipation Proclamation, the papers of the Confederacy, and the Declaration of National Emergency by Reason of Certain Terrorist Attacks, September 14, 2001.

www.infoplease.com

This site has a wealth of information, including an online almanac and atlas and access to *The Columbia Encyclopedia.* The almanac portion of the site provides information in handy tables, such as states' capitals and largest cities, land and water areas of states, population by state (1790–present), national parks and monuments, and states by order of entry into the Union. It also includes geographical information, such as highest, lowest, and mean elevations by state; extreme points of the United States; and mountains and rivers of the U.S. You'll find state profiles, trivia, maps, and flags as well as U.S. documents. Note that this site contains advertisements.

www.bartleby.com

Called "Great Books Online," this site offers a large collection of free online reference books as well as classic works of nonfiction, fiction, and verse. Among its relevant reference works are *The Columbia Encyclopedia, The World Factbook,* and *The Columbia Gazetteer of North America,* an encyclopedia of geographical places and features. Relevant nonfiction works include American historical documents, inaugural addresses, the Lincoln-Douglas debates, and writings by William Penn, Benjamin Franklin, Thomas Paine, Ulysses S. Grant, Booker T. Washington, and Theodore Roosevelt. Note that this site contains advertisements.

www.50states.com

This site is worth your looking at because of the amount of information it gathers in one place. The Fast Facts entry for each state is interesting, with fun facts and trivia. However, the site is not visually appealing and requires finding the information you need from long lists of data irrelevant to most students but perhaps useful to residents. It would be difficult for younger students to navigate. Note that this site contains advertisements.

Subscription-Based Sites

You may have access to excellent subscription-based resources through your school or community library, either in the library or remotely from your own computer. For example, Grolier Online subscriptions are not sold to individuals but are available to schools and libraries. Ask your school or library if they subscribe and whether you can access the sites remotely.

America the Beautiful

America the Beautiful (http://atb.grolier.com/) is the single most helpful resource we've discovered for learning about the fifty states. Available through many libraries and schools, this site has articles, illustrations, photographs, modern and historical maps, and multimedia features focusing on each state and its key cities and attractions. An excellent source for both historical and current information, *America the Beautiful* is written and designed for youth and is attractive and easy to navigate. Photos, maps, and historical paintings bring the text to life. A timeline for each state runs alongside a U.S. timeline, putting key events in context. The site includes biographies of all American presidents and information about major explorers and Native American tribes. United States dependencies are also covered.

Lands and Peoples

The *Lands and Peoples* (http://lp.grolier.com/) subscription site features articles, maps, photographs, and charts about the countries of the world. From the home screen you can choose "Focus: North America," generating the North America home screen and providing you with direct access to the site's coverage of the United States and its regions and states. Coverage includes United States maps showing agriculture, climatic zones, geology, national parks, natural vegetation, population density, precipitation, and temperature. The site's Electronic Atlas is fantastic. In the North America section, historical maps show Indian cultures, the routes of European explorers, the Thirteen Colonies, the French and Indian War, U.S. territorial expansion, the War of 1812, the Texas Revolution, the Mexican War, the U.S. in 1860, Indian wars, the slave trade, and U.S. Immigration (1820–1970). A print version of *Lands and Peoples* has a portion of the site's resources.

American Indian History and Culture

This Facts on File subscription site (http://www.fofweb.com/Onfiles/Indian/default.asp?ItemID=WE43) features articles, biographies, maps, timelines, images, and primary source documents detailing the Native American experience and many related U.S. history topics. This site is an excellent source for older students and for the teacher's own research. The site is easily searchable, with easy-to-follow, interesting cross-references that start a person off on a trail of learning. It is a good source for studying American Indian cultures, U.S.–American Indian relations and policies, the westward expansion of the U.S., Indian wars, the changing Indian Country, etc. It has many excellent maps, including those showing the growth of the United States and Indian land cessions.

History Resource Center: US

This Thomson Gale Infotrac subscription site (http://galenet.galegroup.com) is a good source for articles, biographies, and primary source documents from history journals and reference titles. This site is not designed for children. It is more appropriate for the teacher's own information gathering or for older students.

eLibrary: Maps

This subscription site (http://elibrary.bigchalk.com/libweb/elib/do/login) has maps from magazines, U.S. and foreign newspapers, radio and television news programs, and reference books. This site is not designed for children. It is more appropriate for the teacher's own information gathering or for older students.

Movie

The Scrambled States of America and More Stories to Celebrate Our Country

Producer: Weston Woods
Publication: New York: Scholastic, 2003
ISBN: 0439643899
Description: 1 DVD, 65 minutes, closed captioned (also available as VHS)

Summary: Disenchanted with their fixed places on the map, the states decide to swap spots in hopes that each can get to see a different part of the country and do something different for a change. Recommended for ages four to nine, this video adaptation of the picture book *The Scrambled States of America* (see Books) also includes the stories of "This Land Is Your Land," "The Star-Spangled Banner," John Henry, and Johnny Appleseed.

UNITED STATES

OF AMERICA